To

Lisa (Wife)

On the Occasion of

44TH _Birthday!_

From

Tom (Husband)

BAREFOOT
IN MY HEART

Starting a fresh conversation with God

❦

JILL BRISCOE

MONARCH
BOOKS

Oxford, UK, and Grand Rapids, Michigan, USA

First published in the UK in 2011 by Monarch Books
(a publishing imprint of Lion Hudson plc)
Wilkinson House, Jordan Hill Road, Oxford, OX2 8DR, England
Tel: +44 (0)1865 302750 Fax: +44 (0)1865 302757
Email: monarch@lionhudson.com
www.lionhudson.com

Published in association with the literary agency of Alive Communications, Inc., 7680 Goddard Street, Suite 200, Colorado Springs, CO 80920.
www.alivecommunications.com

ISBN 978 0 85721 033 3

Distributed by:
UK: Marston Book Services, PO Box 269, Abingdon, Oxon, OX14 4YN
USA: Kregel Publications, PO Box 2607, Grand Rapids, Michigan 49501

Picture Acknowledgments
Alamy p. 113 (travelib asia), p. 125 (Rob Walls); Chris Atkinson pp. 35, 94, 99; Bill Bain pp. 19, 53, 102; Alan Brett pp. 26–27, 40; Christine Chouler p. 65; Roger Chouler pp. 6, 22, 31, 51, 58, 63, 69, 70, 89, 107, 109, 127, 129, 134, 149, 158, 169, 173; Corbis p. 79 (Ocean), p. 167 (Hans-Peter Siffert/the food passionates); Chris Hall pp. 14, 76, 83; Len Kerswill pp. 12, 15, 39, 60, 87, 97, 118, 132, 144, 160; Estelle Lobban pp. 10, 45, 57, 59, 93, 117, 121, 138, 142, 151, 157, 165, 171; Kathryn Smith p. 48; iStockphoto p. 42 (Eugene Tomeev); Andy Taylor p. 162–163; Nigel Ward pp. 2–3, 67, 105, 141, 174–175.

British Library Cataloguing Data
A catalogue record for this book is available from the British Library.

Printed and bound in China.

To my dear women friends, examples, mentors, and ministry companions in my UK years: women all, mothers, sisters, daughters, and lovers of Christ. Thank you for you.

Especially:
Janet, who led me thoroughly to faith in a Christ I didn't know but longed to.

Grace, recently promoted to Glory, who corralled a wild new convert and taught her life-saving spiritual disciplines while at college.

Joan, my leader, and model of practical and total surrender to Him, as we worked together in youth mission: joyfully doing His will under constant stress and difficult life circumstances.

And Angie, my closest friend and fellow warrior in the wild days of "reaching, teaching and preaching" in the streets, pubs and dark places of our towns.

Wonderful adventures all! Partners in ministry, but above all, friends after the likes of Ecclesiastes:

Two are better than one, because they have a good return
  for their work:
If one falls down, his friend can help him up. But pity the
  man who falls
and has no one to help him up! ...
Though one may be overpowered, two can defend
  themselves.

Ecclesiastes 4:9–12a

I bless the Lord for you.

Jill

CONTENTS

FOREWORD

*I*N TODAY'S FRENETIC WORLD, a land of iPads and satellite TV, busyness and restlessness seem to be our second nature. We often yearn for a better way, but those longings are so easily crowded out. Here in this volume is a roadmap to a peaceful heart. Jill, drawing on all her years of experience, is a trusted guide. She has trodden the path and her insights are practical, insightful and incredibly genuine. She doesn't flinch from the hard stuff. Her straightforward advice on dealing with anger, self worth, our purpose in life and the difficulties of miracles are all laid bare. Here are words of wisdom drawn from the well of time. Time with the Saviour. I have been blessed and inspired by these writings and you could be too. In order to grow deeper with God, as the book so rightly says: The best way is to begin.

Peter Kerridge

Chief Executive, Premier Media Group

THE "NEARING OF GOD"

*T*ONCE HEARD THAT the Ancients described their experience of the Lord as the "nearing of God".

It reminded me of Jeremiah after his enemies threw him into a pit. In his extremity, the prophet cried out to God to save him. He later testifies, "You came near when I called You, and You said, 'Do not fear'" (Lamentations 3:57). Jeremiah experienced the "nearing of God".

What do we know of this experience of the living God in our desperate moments or in our daily days? He invites each of His children to know Him at a deeper level than we have ever known Him before. It is up to us to take Him up on the invitation and to claim that promise: "Draw near to God, and he will draw near to you" (James 4:8 ESV).

You and I are invited to find God in a deeper measure for ourselves. I pray that this little book will set you off on a grand adventure like nothing you have known before.

Enjoy!

Jill Briscoe

GETTING TO KNOW ME

*H*ELLO, I'M JILL BRISCOE. I'd like to tell you a little about myself. So make a cup of tea, settle down, and enjoy.

I have been in ministry for fifty-six years, a ministry wife for fifty-three last July. I am the wife of a father of three and a grandfather of thirteen; the wife of an ex-banker, and Royal Marine commando. The spouse of a Jesus lover and glory giver, evangelist, youth leader, missionary, author, evangelical leader, preacher and teacher par excellence, a "pastor of pastors" and "minister at large". I am also the wife of a million- (or two-) mile flyer!

My husband Stuart on the other hand has been the husband of a mother of three and a grandmother of thirteen for approximately the same amount of time! He too has been married fifty-three years come July. He would echo the words of a man learning English as a second language, who, in a job application, described himself as: "A much be-childenized gentleman who had sixteen empty stomachs hanging round his neck and couldn't make both his ends meet!"

Stuart, my heart partner and dearest friend, love of my life, has found himself to be the husband of a youth leader and evangelist, teacher, preacher, mentor of women, author and speaker, and, so importantly, mother of three children in ministry and thirteen grandchildren. He, like me, is also the spouse of a "minister at large", and a million- (or two-) mile flyer!

He is also the long-suffering husband of a wife who loses things all over the world. All sorts of things – passports, cars, mobile phones, back rests, Bibles and notes (not copied), and keys are the most common. He told me the other day he was not at all surprised that God gave the keys of the kingdom to Peter and not to Peter's wife! Stuart and I have been on a mission ever since we met. Simply put, we love the Lord and revel in Him. We both signed up for active duty over fifty years ago.

On 9/11, I found myself in Newfoundland along with all my fellow passengers from flight United 929. (We'd been diverted to Canada when the planes hit the Twin Towers in New York.) As we waited in a Salvation Army hall in Gambo, Newfoundland, I discovered that one of my fellow passengers was from the US armed forces, and she was very distressed about being in the army! This had not been the case before the planes crashed and the Twin Towers came down!

Suddenly she burst into tears and sobbed: "I didn't join the army to go to war!"

"Why did you join?" I asked, bewildered.

"To get a fully paid education," she answered without hesitation. "I never anticipated having to fight."

I thought about that a lot in the six days it took us to get home.

We – Stuart and I – joined the army too: His. But we joined to go to war: God's. We declared loud and clear we wanted to honour God, preach the Word, love the people, and make the devil sorry he started the whole mess in the first place.

We have had a ministry marriage that has had its fair share of challenges, joys and sorrows. When we launched out on this grand adventure, this laughing life, this incredibly stretching project, we determined that the ethos of our marriage and family would be service. We agreed: "As for me and my house 'we' will serve the Lord." "We" would serve. Not He would serve or She or They but *We*. We would be an undivided family with one aim in this regard.

If God in grace gifted us with a believing family, each of us would pay whatever price was needed to achieve our goal — to make His heart smile, to experience His kiss on our cheek, His light in our eyes, His work in our hands. *This* is what our family would be about.

We have had the privilege of serving the Lord in mission and church on all seven continents! Amazing! And now at the age of seventy-six I have too much of His business to attend to for months ahead to waste energy worrying about what *might* be. I take courage from looking back at His faithfulness, looking around at the challenge of the work yet to be accomplished, and looking forward to a sprint to the finishing line. There will be battles to come but remember, we *did* join the army to go to war!

I have taken every aspect of my "Wifedom" and "Motherdom" seriously. That is not to say I have always been a successful wife! I have, I am afraid to say (but I must!), been a whiny wife, an impatient wife, a discontented wife, an angry, tired and discouraged wife, a frightened and a timid wife. In the same vein, I have been so very often a less than adequate mother and grandmother too.

In earlier days I struggled with my identity. At our church at first, I resented always being introduced as "the pastor's wife". "Don't these people know my parents gave me a really nice name?" I would mutter into my coffee cup. "After all," I would gripe, "they don't address Mrs Smith as the park director's or zoo keeper's wife! I have a name. I am a person with gifts to offer, a heart to care, and a life to love away!"

I have handled criticism of my husband and children poorly, and whined when Stuart put the *other* family first. (We have two families, don't we? The church family and our own?) I have hidden behind a fake smile while saying sweetly: "So glad you could make it to church today, Mrs Gossip. Do come back." I have prayed too little, talked too much, doubted God could ever make me a blessing, been unwilling to do things badly as I learned to do them well, and struggled with expectations – the church's, my husband's and my own.

I have resisted change, wrestled with loneliness, and lack of friends and resources. I have put on some of the best "pity parties" in town and pouted when nobody I'd invited showed up.

I understand the meaning of the word "stretched". Paul says he was "stretched but never snapped" (2 Corinthians 4:8, my translation) and I too, in my small way, testify that His divine energy given to me has been equal to the task. He does indeed equip the called (not, as someone has said, call the equipped)!

"It's a great life if you don't weaken!" the novelist and historian John Buchan once said; I know there's no fear of that. I am a wife who knows full well what it is both to *run on* and to *run out*! Run out of energy, sleep, health, safety, wealth, friends, trust, peace, and joy. But I am here to tell you too, I am a ministry wife who *has never run out of God*.

So I am writing this in an English spring, in the midst of the hills just south of England's Lake District replete with Wordsworth's golden daffodils "fluttering and dancing in the breeze". I am at Capernwray Bible School and Conference Centre. It's a place that played a significant part in our lives when our family lived here working in the "army".

Early one morning, after a nostalgic walk in the beautiful parklands around the big castle that is Capernwray, I spent time with Him who is my life and wrote this:

Hey, world,
Help yourself to my life,
It is yours.
Help yourself to my love,
It is His!
Help yourself to my time: Jesus taught me I can't keep hours
like the post office!
Welcome to my heart.
Make yourself at home:
Let's have a cup of tea!

Why don't you get your Bible, journal, and your heart! Let's have
a cup of tea!

Jill
April 2011

MAKING A START

∽

I F YOU WANT TO START A HABIT, the best way to begin is to begin! This little volume really is just a starter. Let me help you establish a life-transforming relationship with God by suggesting some ways to read, mark, meditate on and inwardly digest the Word of God, develop your prayer skills, and memorize Scripture. Alternatively, let me encourage you to restart an old discipline that has fallen on hard times.

So let's start at the very beginning. Read Genesis 1:1–5.

At the beginning of time, there was chaos and it was dark.

Is your life chaotic? Does God need to "hover" over the chaos in your life and bring some semblance of order to things? Things that have to do with you and God? With you and other people? You and the church? You and your circumstances? Is it dark inside your personal world? Do you need light to dispel the deep shadows?

God's Word can do that. Just as He did right at the beginning of time when the Word was spoken and there was light and life where none had been before, so God's creative work can be accomplished in our hearts today. Invite Him who made the worlds to remake your inner world.

All you need to do is begin the conversation and say the following prayer:

"Lord, I need a 'Genesis moment'.
A new start to my day,
A new light to my way.
My heart is talking, Lord. Are you listening?"

"You are clearly heard. In fact, before you spoke, I knew
the words on your tongue altogether."

Shine on me, Lord God Almighty, Maker of heaven and
earth. Bring order out of chaos. Chase the shadows of
darkness back into the nether world. Make of me a new
creation in Christ Jesus. Give me a Genesis moment,
Lord!

Amen

"There was evening and there was morning – the first day"

Something Out of Nothing

On the first day, God did a whole new thing. He made something out of the nothing. Where there was a void, He filled it. Where there was no substance or form, He created shapes, colour, and reality – with deep beauty. And even after one day – one evening and morning of Genesis moments – the world was changed forever!

Struggling?

Do you constantly struggle to find a way in which *your* world can be changed forever? A Genesis moment? Do you long for God to speak into your life in such a way that you would know things would never be the same again? Maybe you have been a believer for a long time but this personal devotional time when you are meant to meet with God has eluded you. Have you tried *this* method and *that* method of having a meaningful "Quiet Time" with God and given up through lack of discipline, frustration, or discouragement, because it seemed to make no difference? What did it matter if you read your Bible or not, or whether you prayed for two minutes, ten minutes, or an hour?

How many good resolutions have you broken concerning your devotional intentions? And yet you know deep down that this is the secret of all things real. To hear His voice bringing substance into the void in your heart and experience the power of the living Word chasing darkness out of your soul, enlightening the mind, is all joy!

Perhaps it has not been your experience to see prayers fulfilled or to hear the praise of angels in "the deep place where nobody goes". How would you like a new day to dawn? Like the very first of all days: like a "Genesis day"?

Try another format to "refresh" your time with the Lord. In the morning, try a reading of the Word with application to your life; a meditation or memorization arising out of the "morning Word" at break-time; and an evening prayer "adventure" based on

the day's overall theme.

This can start a pattern of practising "thinking of Scripture", reminding yourself of what perhaps you may have forgotten, and turning the application of what you read into prayer in order to bless yourself and your world.

The Best Way to Begin is to Begin

I suggest you begin right now. Read, study, think, pray, praise, meditate, write, or memorize. Do one or all! Take as little or much time as you want. There are many different sorts of devotions in this book, and from these devotions you can develop many more! One thing may lead you to explore another. Connect with God in prayer and ask the Holy Spirit to help you understand His Holy Word. That's His job.

I would suggest taking as much time as you *can* each day. It could be five, ten, or sixty minutes. Whatever! You decide. Start with a minimum and grow into it.

After you have been practising some simple, tried and tested Bible study and prayer habits, you can create your own. You could even write your own devotional for your children, friends, parents and church! That would be fun! You can begin at any time of the year, or on any date. Use a journal or notebook to record your discoveries, and capture your own conversations with the Lord.

Time to start a habit!

LIFE LESSONS

HORTLY AFTER I CAME TO a living faith in Christ, I discovered that I had some responsibilities to fulfil in my relationship with God.

The first lesson I learned is that I am responsible for looking after my own interior life. I need to be intentional in this endeavour.

This was worth "a conversation" with the Lord, don't you think?

> "Lord," I began, "You mean I need to take responsibility to grow my own soul? You won't do that for me?"
>
> "It takes two," He answered.
>
> "It doesn't just automatically happen once I've invited your Holy Spirit into my heart?"
>
> "There are rules that make it work."
>
> "There are rules to our relationship?"
>
> "Of course!"
>
> "Like what?"
>
> "You need to plan to spend time with me."
>
> "It sounds sort of 'unspiritual' to – to have – like – a plan! Doesn't it just happen inside you without you doing anything?" (I'd rather hoped it did, you know. I knew the answer to that, of course!)

After our talk, I spent a bit of time in the "garden of grace", on "the steps of my soul", just thinking about it. I considered other relationships in my life. They didn't just happen. They needed work! So wouldn't the most important relationship of all take work too? Holy work! Somehow "Holy" and "work" didn't seem right either! God work! I thought. What a privilege and how exciting! A poem came to me:

> *I revel in Your beauty and I celebrate Your peace,*
> *And as I am obedient, I find such sweet release.*
> *I'm passionate to please you and live a life of praise*
> *So I'll smile at dark tomorrows and sanctify my days.*
>
> *Ever climbing upward and reaching for a star,*
> *I know no sense of loneliness for I know where you are;*
> *You're living in my ransomed soul, You're filling every day*
> *So I'll lose myself in loving and I'll give myself away.*
>
> *I revel in your presence and I celebrate Your grace,*
> *And I want to stay forever and look into Your face.*
> *But now is time for serving and I need to do my part,*
> *So go with me, Lord Jesus, and fill my needy heart!*

I began to spend some minutes every day celebrating our relationship – revelling in Him. I read His Word and prayed: the two essentials to grow your soul. But for this to happen I needed to have a spiritual schedule.

IT ALL TAKES PRACTICE

THE SECOND LESSON I LEARNED is that I need to be responsible to practise this intentional spiritual relationship with God on a daily basis and not waste one single day! Don't waste time. We don't know how many days we have for our discoveries!

So, to help myself, I get my calendar out and look at each day in the coming week. Then I block off thirty minutes each day at the best time for practising my spiritual growth (it could be a different time every day). I put the appointment on my schedule. Then I keep myself accountable to keep it. Then I get excited. (Blessed is she that expecteth nothing, she shall not be disappointed!) After all of that – I enjoy!

So how does a conversation with God develop? Like this.

Read a passage from the Bible

Just pick one, for example, Philippians 3.

Comment on the passage

Even after many years of immersing myself in God's word, I often find it helpful to use one of the many Bible resources that are available. Some of the thoughts that follow were gleaned from a Bible commentary, that is to say, a book that "comments" on the text. I put the comments into *my own* words, which made me think about the meaning and not just "parrot" someone else's thoughts.

This is what I came up with:

For Paul, the great apostle, the knowledge of Christ Jesus meant knowing Him interiorly. The intimate communion with Christ that started at his conversion and had been his ongoing joy and experience all his years, was not just for the past, (see verse 10), but was a growing thing, in which there was the challenge and the excitement of increasing understanding of Christ in the most personal of ways. When you receive Christ, this is only the beginning of your discovery of Him. What riches this entails. To search them out and appropriate them personally takes a lifetime. Paul said, "I want to know Him, and I want to know him more."

Then I applied this truth to my own life. I "sat my soul down" and asked it some hard questions.

Do I want to know Him more? Then I'll tell Him right there, right then!

> *"Lord, I do want to know You in ways I've never experienced before."*

I make a plan to "home school" myself, and for this I need both a Bible plan and a prayer plan! I need to listen to His words, and respond in faith and obedience. Then I need to learn to intercede, until I know how to be "formidable on my knees for God".

After this I usually sit still and quiet, and after a while talk with Him:

"Lord of Life, keep me faithful in doing these most important of exercises. I need perseverance to do my part. Even to just show up! It shouldn't be too hard but somehow it is!"

"That's because Satan doesn't want you and I to meet," I heard Him say, *"to talk, to dialogue about our relationship. He would disrupt this at all times, and by all means."*

"I remember a little couplet, Lord:

'The devil trembles when he sees

The weakest saint upon his knees.'"

"Yes, indeed he does!" He said, very seriously. *"He knows, when you and I meet, that you are linked to the very power of God. The power that alone is bent on his deserved destruction."*

"Sort of scary!"

"What is the alternative, Jill?"

"Not to talk to You, and make him happy?

"Well, that's one alternative!"

"But Lord, I know better than to talk to him. That is the path to sure and certain misery!"

"True."

"And to talk and listen to You is the sure and certain path to joy unspeakable!"

"That's true too!"

"O Lord, thank you for the priceless privilege of such sacred conversations. Help me to keep them up!"

Try the following passages to help you make a start.

From the Old Testament

- Psalm 1
- Psalm 37:1–11
- Isaiah 53

From the New Testament

- Luke 4:14–21
- 1 John 1
- 2 Peter 1:3–10

A Bible commentary can be so helpful when you don't have much knowledge of the Bible or its background. Visit a Christian bookstore and ask to see some evangelical commentaries or other books to help you dig deeper into God's word. Ask their advice about the benefits of each book. Build a bookshelf of "help" books – your very own library.

BLESSINGS BEFORE BREAKFAST

*S*OMEHOW, EARLY MORNING conversations with God seem particularly blessed!

Read Mark 1:35–39. Use your Bible and journal.

Ask questions of the text. Look for the answers in the passage. This is one way of having a devotional time with the Lord. It's a way someone taught me when I was first converted to Christ.

Answer the questions first yourself without looking at my findings. Always pray about what you have learned and share the blessing.

You can use the words *Who, What, Where, When, Why,* and *How* throughout the passage as I have. You can do this "solo" or with a parent, child, sibling, friend, or with a group. I've given you a verse reference as a clue in some places but left you to find the rest yourself.

- Who is this about?
- Where did this occur? (See verse 21.)
- What had happened the previous day? Describe this.
- When did Jesus get up and go?
- How early? (See verse 35.)
- Where did Jesus go to? (See verse 35.)
- What do you think Jesus wanted to do and did He do it?

- When his disciples found Him, what do you think He and His Father had been talking about? (See verse 38.) Think about this.

Now, to give your discoveries some context, look up Isaiah 61:1–3, which talks about the coming Messiah. What has he been anointed to do?

- From the verses in Isaiah, make a list in your journal of all the prophet said about what the Messiah would do when He came. How many things did you find?

My Discoveries

This is what I found and noted. Jesus has just begun His ministry and has been up very late healing people. A great crowd has gathered around the door of the house where He was staying – Peter's house in Capernaum. Everyone has had a very short night.

This was "very early" (verse 35) before anyone else is stirring in the house. Before breakfast. My thought: "Up early, even though the day preceding this very early appointment had been full of extraordinary doings of the supernatural kind, impacting His body, soul and spirit, and He must have been very tired."

I think Jesus had been talking with His Father about His calling to redeem the world. Success and lots of people excited about His ministry didn't always mean that Jesus allowed that to drive His agenda. He needed to go to the "little towns and villages," too.

Personal Application

If possible, find a place where you won't be disturbed till your business with God is done (verse 37). Pray about one thing you got out of these Scriptures today. Have a "conversation" with God about it. This was mine:

> *"Lord, I don't do 'early' easily!"*
> *"I know."*
> *"I need to, though."*
> *"Yes you do."*
> *"How did you do it when you were as tired as you were?"*
> *"That's what servants do. What has 'tired' got to do with it?"*
> *"Er, nothing really…"*

Then I remembered a chorus I learned over fifty years ago. We used to sing it in our youth meetings.

> *"In the morning first of all*
> *Saviour let me hear Thy call.*
> *Make me ready to obey*
> *Thy commands throughout the day."*

BLESSINGS BEFORE BREAKFAST

I determined to be a good servant.

The next day I got up "very early"; He was waiting for me. After a while, I sang Him the little song I had remembered and went out into my busy day. I was tired but it was worth it.

Share this blessing with a friend, group, or someone in your family. Maybe you could tell others some of the things you and the Lord talked about, especially the application of His Word from this passage. Don't wait until you see them next – use an email, text or tweet.

Think about it during the day. PRAY about whom to share it with. Don't forget to set your alarm half an hour earlier when you go to bed tonight. You have an early appointment tomorrow.

BAREFOOT IN MY HEART

EARLY BIRD

"THE EARLY BIRD ALWAYS GETS THE WORM," or so they say! So one day, "this bird" committed to get up very early and go and look for nourishment. Food for me – for you.

This would be apart and different from some of the other ways I feed my soul, which take more time and of course must not be neglected. Today I determined that what I would find (or "dig up") early in the morning, I would pass on to at least one other person during the day. I would simply enjoy the meal the Bird Maker provided and then let other people know the location of my discovery. It would not only be for me but for others too!

It was at this moment that I realized how self-centred I had sometimes been in my personal communion with God! It had really only been about me and mine! I hadn't thought too much about passing on the blessings to others. How horrible! *"Sorry Lord!"*

When I asked the Bird Maker to *whom* I should send this early information as a blessing, He replied that He would tell me day by day. This would require quiet moments at the conclusion of the enjoyment of my own discoveries to allow Him to bring the right person or people to mind. How exciting! Think about it, I *could be a blessing before breakfast!* Fun!

I purposed to rise a little earlier than usual. Spreading my

wings the next morning I took off from my cosy bed branch keeping my eyes open, my soul expectant and my heart ready for a good result! I knew I would not be disappointed.

Listening to my thoughts, He who loves all His birds reminded me with a smile, "Don't forget, 'the early bird always gets the worm'!"

Try it! Do it for a week. Buy a packet of nice blank cards and each day pen your "early blessings" to send to someone.

GIVING GRACE

"And there were shepherds…
and a light shone round about them."
Luke 2:8–9, paraphrased

❧

It's all right to read the Christmas narrative "off Christmas!" What a shame to think about the giving Grace of God the Father only as we celebrate the wonderful gift of His "One and Only" to the human race. Read John 1:1–14, or Luke's Christmas story many times during the year, to remind yourself of the incredible miracle of the incarnation. If you'd been one of the shepherds, would you ever have stopped telling your incredible story, or reserved it for once a year?

The Word made flesh came to a place
In Bethlehem, through giving Grace,
Some shepherds and some poor folk there,
Who came to kneel, or stand and stare,
Remarked the very stars seemed bright,
Especially one – that Christmas night.

The light shone piercing darkness deep;
It seemed that men were fast asleep.

Yet shepherds few, though rough and poor,
Directed to a stable door,
Believed the message Gabriel gave
Of God Almighty come to save.

So what do you believe of Him
Who came that night to Bethlehem?
If He is God as angels said
Then why come to that stable bed?
Perhaps so sinners see His Grace
The light of God upon His face?

So come and worship Him that came
And you will never be the same!
Once we have worshipped Him this night,
Let's be for Him His little light:
For you and me the Father lost
His Christmas child at such a cost!

Maybe you could read this or another Christmas carol, hymn or poem when you have your family Christmas party this year?

When you share this with others, try to engage them in the all-important dialogue: "Who *was* the baby in the manger?" Were the shepherds really in a conspiracy to dupe the world? If not, isn't it rather amazing that they left their sheep (not a good idea if they valued their jobs), and more amazing still, that they actually found a baby in a trough, the baby who was the reason they risked their livelihood and "came to see".

GIVING GRACE

GOD OF PERFECT TIMING

"When the time had fully come,
God sent His Son born of a woman…".
Galatians 4:4

God of perfect timing, Word of wisdom rare,
Eternal God incredible to see you sleeping there.
How can it be, dear Lord of life, You came to tell us all,
Our only hope of heaven lay within that cattle stall?

Many ways to Jesus, seekers take to find,
Many people looking for a Saviour for mankind.
Many different wonderings, for many want to know,
Just "who" was born at Bethlehem, a long time ago?

Was He just a good man, a teacher, kind and true?
Or was it God who came to earth to save a chosen few?
Was it all a story, improbable and wild,
Or God that day, in bed of hay, a tiny, human child?

What do I know of Jesus and His changing, saving grace?
What difference is there in my life: has Christmas taken
place?

BAREFOOT IN MY HEART

How dare I live a selfish life when God gave His for me?
The choice is mine, and now's the time, to let Him set me
*   free!*

So Christmas now this season could be a different thing,
This year I could accept Him, and hear the angels sing.
So as I bow, right here, right now, and call upon His name,
My world, because of Christmas – will never be the same.

Having read the poem, stay still and quiet. Enjoy the silence. Think about the last verse of the poem. Has "Christmas" happened in your life? Do you want to borrow my words and invite the living Lord Jesus into your life?

Lord of life, Light of the world: I believe. I believe you are
God. I believe you were born at Bethlehem: a Saviour for
the world from sin and its consequences. Be "my" Saviour,
Lord Jesus. Enter my life by your Holy Spirit. Forgive
"my" sin, Lord. May your Spirit tell my spirit You are in
my soul as You promised. Thank you, Lord.

Amen

ॐ

GOD OF PERFECT TIMING

If you sincerely prayed this prayer, tell someone that you did. Then be like the shepherds who "when they had seen Him, spread the word concerning what they had been told about the child." Tell your Bethlehem; "a Saviour has been born to you, He is Christ the Lord!"

LIKE A WATERED GARDEN

"HE WHO REFRESHES OTHERS WILL HIMSELF BE REFRESHED."

Proverbs 11:25

❧

A BIBLE PROMISE THAT HAS encouraged me all my life is: "The Lord will guide you always; He will satisfy your needs in a sun-scorched land and will strengthen your frame. You will be like a well-watered garden, like a spring whose waters never fail" (Isaiah 58:11).

Let's dig a bit deeper.

The Context

This was a promise for the people of God when they had come home after exile in Babylon. A promise that their lives would be "like a well-watered garden" (Jeremiah 31:12), always refreshed and ever refreshing others – flourishing under God's blessing – and all their sorrows would be over.

The Consequences

I have found, as Solomon said, "…He who refreshes others will himself be refreshed" (Proverbs 11:25). This is what I want my life to be like, so that people will come to me and ask, "Can I walk around the garden of your life and be refreshed?" For this I must discipline myself to make sure there is plenty of living water flowing all over my life!

The Challenge

What about you? Are you a blessing to others? Remember, the water of life is a picture of the Holy Spirit – Jesus said so in John 4:10, 13 and John 7:38. Is the Living Water flowing?

Look up these two passages – John 4:4–30; John 7:25–39 – and read about the two events. Ask yourself the following questions:
- What did Jesus say about Himself?
- What did Jesus say to the woman?
- What did Jesus say to the crowd in the temple?

Do you believe Him? Talk to Him about what you've discovered.

> *Like a watered garden, fresh as morning dew,*
> *New and fragrant, where the vagrant,*
> *Homeless soul, who thirsts for You,*
> *Comes to rest and comes to see*
> *The Christ I love refreshing me!*

Walk among the flowers, growing in His Grace;
May you know and may you grow
Blooms of beauty in this place.
Watered blossoms, Spirit-sown
By Christ of God beside His throne.

- Using a concordance, look up a few references where water is used as an illustration.

- Which of these is your favourite passage? Why?

- Record today's spiritual lesson or insights in your journal.

LIKE A WATERED GARDEN

BLESSINGS AT BREAK-TIME

*W*HAT HAPPENS IF ON ONE OR TWO DAYS you don't get up early enough to receive a "Blessing before Breakfast?" Use your coffee or tea break instead. Or you could even spend time with the Lord before you go to sleep. Although it doesn't seem right to give God our attention at the sleepiest time of our day, it's allowed! Be flexible. You can even split your time with the Lord and meet with Him twice in a day!

Here's the story of my break-time blessing one day when travelling overseas meant I didn't have time in the early hours. I did without lunch in order to do it. That's called "fasting".

Doing the "Do nots"

I had just written a booklet on worry. It was helping a lot of people and I was glad. I was reminded of this, however, as I eventually got a breathing space in a busy travel day. I had a lot to worry about and was busy mentally working my way through all my concerns. Conscious of this I decided to read about worrying. It's good to know your Bible so well you know just where to turn when a certain topic is needed. So I read Matthew 6, remembering that this was the well-known chapter where Jesus talks about worry. In fact, I call it "the worry-not chapter". I had read it many times

and, as I said, had actually written a little booklet about how not to worry, yet I now mused that I should probably read it again! The older you get, you know, the more times you need to remind yourself of what Jesus said about a subject, and the older I get the more booklets on worry I need to write!

So that day at break-time I found myself sitting in an airport lounge, waiting to fly to the other side of the world and reading Matthew 6. I was struck with how negative Jesus seemed to be! There were so many "do nots!"

We automatically think of "no" as negative don't we? But as I thought about it a bit, I knew that Jesus was saying we have to be negative about some things in our thinking in order to be positive!

Let me highlight some of His "do nots" from Matthew 6 for you. You can join me in my discoveries and write the answers in your journal.

- When you give to the needy, *do not*: a) verse 2; b) verse 3.
- When you pray, *do not*: verse 7.
- When you forgive, *do not*: verse 15.
- When you fast, *do not*: verse 16. (Notice there's a "*will not*" in the same verse!)
- When you store up treasure, *do not*: verse 19.

I kept thinking about this passage of Scripture. I was interrupted many times that travel day but was still able to keep picking up my conversation with the Lord where I left off.

Later that evening at my destination, I settled into my room and picked up the conversation again as I got into bed. It turned out it was the next lot of "do nots" in the passage that especially got to me that day. "DO NOT WORRY" it says in verse 25. Oh dear! How would I know what *not* to worry about? I needn't have worried because there is a list.

Do not worry about:

- Your life (you can't add or subtract one birthday!)

- What to eat and drink.

- What to wear.

Then there's an example of the birds who *do not* worry but let God do the worrying for them: "So do not worry, saying, 'What shall we eat?' or 'What shall we drink?' or 'What shall we wear?'" (verse 31). Three reasons:

- Pagans worry like this and you are not a pagan.

- Our Heavenly Father already knows our needs (not our wants – our needs).

- Our kingdom work – the reason He has left us in this worried world – will be hampered if we are anxious.

I got to the end of the chapter and there it was *again*, "Therefore DO NOT WORRY about TOMORROW, for tomorrow will worry about itself. Each day has enough trouble of its own."

My eye wandered on to Matthew 7, which starts with a "do not", about judging others, but I had enough to keep me going for the rest of my troubled evening!

So how do you and I *not do* the "do nots?"

Consider the birds! Get on with building your nest, hatching your eggs, watching out for predators, singing a song, and generally flying around in grand abandon to the will of God you know for each day. And every time you begin to *do* a "do not" – DON'T! Stop wherever you are and whisper, "I won't go *there* in my mind. I'll go to the promises of God instead: my Heavenly Father 'knows'." And then sing on.

So, *you* mind your mind and *God* will mind your heart.

And so at last, I laid my head on the pillow of that promise and fell fast asleep. Trust will do that for you, you know.

❧

Take a look at Philippians 4:4–9 to read about a final "do not". Hold on to this: "Do not be anxious about anything, but in everything, by prayer and petition, with thanksgiving, present your requests to God... And the God of peace will be with you" (Philippians 4:6,9).

- What are your three biggest worries at the moment? Write them down in your journal.

- Share the biggest one with a friend and ask her or him to pray for you.
- Invite your friend to share their biggest worry with you. Tell her or him you promise to pray about it.
- Don't forget when God answers your prayer to thank your prayer-partner friend.

LOVE YOUR LIFE AWAY

"LOVE NEVER FAILS."

1 Corinthians 13:8

THIS DOES NOT MEAN, OF COURSE, that love never fails to get a response! It means, it never fails to go on loving whether it gets a response or not!

Read 1 Corinthians 13. Read it in three different translations. The different versions may give you new insights into the text.

We have a choice. What is it to be?

> *So what's the choice to be?*
> *To live and die for Him*
> *Who chose to die upon the cross*
> *For selfishness and sin?*
> *Live a dying life*
> *Give away the gold,*
> *Spend myself for Kingdom things*
> *Until I get too old?*
>
> *Or*
> *Keep my life for me,*
> *Pamper and invest*
> *In all the little luxuries*

BAREFOOT IN MY HEART

My selfish self wants best?
Chloroform my conscience
Refuse to face the fact
I've chosen to be self-absorbed
And keep my life intact?

Or
Love my life away
Give my time to Him
Live in glad obedience
Be sensitive to sin.
Count the moments precious
He gives to use each day
Nestle in my Father's arms and
Love my life away.

Love my life away
Pray until I see
Answers to a world in chains
That needs to be set free.
Live a dying life
The self-surrendered way
Enduring cheerfully to the end
And love my life away!

LOVE YOUR LIFE AWAY

My choice:
I'll run the race for Jesus
Until the final day,
And hear Him say, "Well done, my child,
You loved your life away!"

- What is *your* choice? Record it in your journal.
- Who do you need to "go on loving"? Write their name in your journal or in your Bible beside 1 Corinthians 13. Pray for them.
- Read 1 Corinthians 13:4–6 and pray through these verses for the person whose name you have written down. I have written the first couple of sentences for you; use your words to complete the prayer.

Lord, help me to be patient and kind, however people treat me. Help me to think of others before myself… and so on.

TAKING CARE OF BUSINESS

*T*WAS ON A PLANE RETURNING from ministry in the UK and Germany. About 150 women had gathered in Stuttgart for a four-day conference. They were Christian leaders from many different nations. The women included many that I had served with in the past – from Eastern and Western Europe, Dubai and Singapore, and some were from the US military base. There were even two women who had been in Stuart's and my church in the past and others from our current state of Wisconsin! It was a great encouragement to hear the way God had used them in their different service opportunities. We met in the international church where the pastor's wife, a great speaker I'd met in Singapore years ago, had convened the meetings for those who wanted to know how better to grow their ministries.

How could they better evangelize different cultures, and then disciple and train them to disciple others? How could they better reach and rescue trafficked women, the handicapped and mentally challenged, and find ways to work with women of very diverse cultures and religions? These women were key in their ministries already but they came to learn how to be better at what they did for the Lord, and they all came to renew and refresh their own hearts. When you are giving out and giving out you need to pause in order to replenish your own soul. The privilege was mine to bring the plenary message. It was a real blessing to me, but then, "he who refreshes others will himself be refreshed" (Proverbs 11:25)!

The interesting part of it to me was that what they asked me to address in Stuttgart was not something new or deep, or some modern, clever method of evangelism or mission strategy, but rather, "How can *we* stay fresh and vital in our relationship with Christ so we can bless others?" And so we went back to basics and reminded ourselves of the essentials of being "*a spring whose waters never fail*". "How do you do that over the long haul?" they asked me. "What keeps *you* going, Jill? How can we finish strong?"

It is my conviction that we who know Jesus often don't need to learn anything new – we just need to be reminded of what we know very well already! If we all got back to basics: knowing and loving God, we could each become formidable for Christ and His cause. In other words, each of us just needs to "take care of business" – to continue the Holy work of maintaining our relationship with God and keeping our faith vibrant and fresh.

And so we went back to basics and reminded ourselves of the essentials of being "a spring whose waters never fail". Reflecting on this, I took myself to "the steps of my soul". This was worth "a conversation" with the Lord, don't you think?

> *"So Lord, You mean I need to take some sort of action to stay fresh?"*
> *"You already know that, Jill. Remember, I am the water of Life. Come often to this knowledge in your mind."*

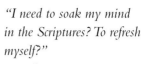

"I need to soak my mind in the Scriptures? To refresh myself?"

"Yes."

"I can do that!"

"Do it then."

"Then what?"

"Overflow!"

"How do I do that?"

"Keep your heart and mind refreshed in my Spirit, and filled to overflowing. Just live your life taking care of business, Jill, and see what happens!"

"Yes!"

"Let's go!"

I read His word and prayed, letting Him freshen my mind and fill my soul, and then walked into a dry and dreary world to overflow and bless others.

Finally, let me show you – from my own life – three key practices that continue to be important to my spiritual growth.

TAKING CARE OF BUSINESS

Be practical

I get my calendar or schedule out. I look at the coming week and block off thirty minutes each day for my "God-time". I plan it. Make an appointment. Then keep it! Then I get excited, and enjoy!

Be spiritual

First, I spend some minutes celebrating Him every day. I read His Word and pray: the two essentials to spiritual growth. For this to happen I need to have a spiritual schedule, with time set aside to read and pray.

Be vertical and horizontal

This applies to my relationships with God and with others. After spending time with Him I may need to share what He's told me with those I meet.

Lord, I will begin! Yes, I will. See me now, making plans:
taking care of business! It's exciting just getting practical.
Teach me, Lord, who You are and what you want of me.
Help me to respond.

Amen

❧

Pass on the blessings you have received today. Think of the person who needs to hear about them and the best way for you to share things with them.

THINGS THAT ARE PRECIOUS TO ME

*T*HAVE BEEN TOLD that when Maria, wife of Hudson Taylor, founder of the China Inland Mission, was with her husband on the mission field, their son was at a missionary school on the other side of the country. One day the bad news came that the Japanese had invaded China and captured the school in which her son lived. There was no news about the well-being or otherwise of the children. Apparently, it wasn't possible to leave the responsibilities she and her husband were charged with to find out the fate of the children – and so she fell to her knees (wouldn't you!?). She said the Lord told her, *"You look after the things that are precious to Me, and I'll look after the things that are precious to you!"*

I wrote the quote in my journal, and many a time (in not nearly such dramatic circumstances), I have used her words to encourage myself.

I have come to experience peace about what is happening at home while I'm literally at the other end of the world: I have been able to get on with the tasks at hand for the church and mission – the reason I'm far away from those I love – with the inner assurance that He is "taking care of business" back home.

However, earlier last year, receiving news that all was not well "back at the ranch", I found the old familiar panic coming back. I

was in the middle of a hectic schedule but went into "trust mode", knowing He knew I was looking after the ministry – *the things that were precious to Him* – while He took care of my stuff – *the things that were precious to me* – far away.

When the conference was over, I suddenly felt unsafe. Now the speaking and training and counselling work were done and it was time for the long journey home. I had finished looking after *the things that were precious to Him,* so I reasoned maybe He must have finished *looking after the things that were precious to me* back home! So I took to worrying about them all over again. No wonder I felt fearful and "unsafe"!

I couldn't sleep that night and I wished I was still speaking and working hard on the missionary work! It was time to have a "conversation".

> *"Lord, I feel very 'unsafe'. I was fine when I knew you were looking after the things at home while I did what you'd asked me to do for you abroad. But now – this hovering apprehension that something really bad is going to go wrong because I've taken back the responsibility of 'being God' is killing me. I'm not as good as you looking after precious things!"*
>
> *"That's because you're not God," He said mildly! "But Jill, the things at home that are precious to you are the things that are precious to me too! Everything that belongs to you matters to me – not just ministry things."*

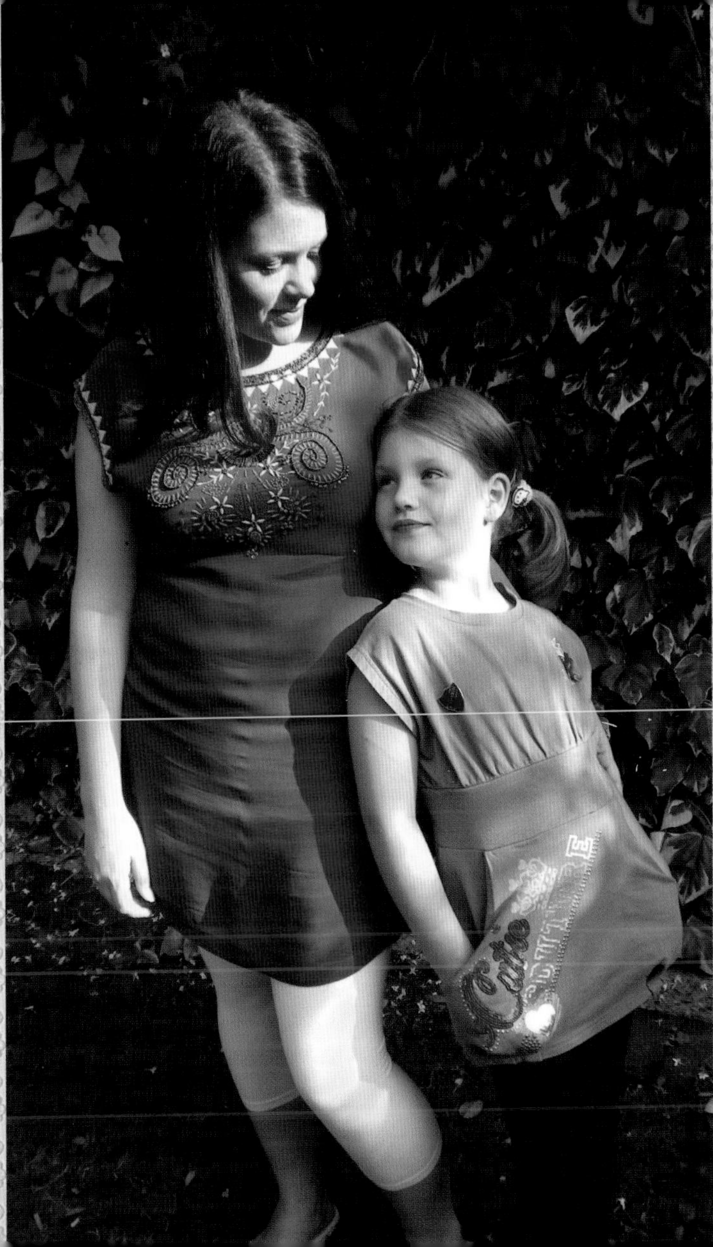

Then peace settled my spirit down! Of course! How stupid I had been. It's *all* precious to Him! I can trust Him to be taking care of business – my business – whether I'm at home or abroad!

"Thank you, Lord!"

What a life lesson. The difference is that He is God and I am not. I'm really glad about that!

Spend a little time thanking Him for "taking care of business", whatever you are doing (or not doing) for Him in your ministry and family. Your family IS your ministry too, isn't it?

BAREFOOT IN MY HEART

WORSHIPPING WORRY AWAY

Are you obsessed with worry? Have you tried praying and giving your worries to God but they won't go? They seem stuck to your heart like Velcro! Then worship! Offer Him your prayers and praise and give Him permission to take your load of worry. It's almost impossible to worry when your heart knows He is near, closer than breathing.

Sometimes it helps to read a really familiar verse of Scripture in different versions or paraphrases of the Bible. It can give you new insights into His Word. Try this out with some beloved and familiar verses from the book of Philippians: "Instead of worrying, pray. Let your petitions and praises shape your worries into prayers, letting God know your concerns. Before you know it, a sense of God's wholeness, everything coming together for good, will come and settle you down" (Philippians 4:6–7, *The Message*).

Reading His Book always focuses your attention on Him, and worship helps us to stay still enough for our agitated hearts to be filled with "the peace of God, which surpasses all understanding" (Philippians 4:7, NKJV). Only Jesus can do this for us. Do you feel stretched tight as a drum? Is life worrying you silly? Try staying still long enough to be conscious of the nearness of God. The battle against obsessive worry can go on a long time. It has for me.

Recently, I came across this poem I'd penned after some

"worshipping worry away" time with the Lord.

I'm not a knot Lord, no I'm not,
Well, not at the moment.
Keep me untied, Lord,
Straighten me out
Take hold of the frayed ends,
Hold them securely in place.
Help me lie still in your hands while You tease out the
  tightness.

Tied in tight against myself,
Twisted over
In knots of knot-ness,
I'm no good to You, or me, or the people I love.
Help me, Lord, not to be a knot!

Amen

Do you want to add a verse of your own? Or maybe if you worship for a while, you can write a poem too?

THE BOY

⟨ornament⟩

*I*T HAD BEEN A GREAT PRIVILEGE to be with over a hundred
people from different continents, experiencing some of the Holy
Land – its rich history, archaeology, and biblical record. Stuart and
me, plus Pete, our youngest son, and his family were travelling
together. We shared the ministry, applying what we learned at sites
such as the Sea of Galilee, the Mount of Beatitudes, the Pools of
Bethsaida and Siloam (in Jerusalem), Jericho, Bethlehem, Nazareth,
and, of course, Gethsemane, Calvary, and the Garden Tomb!

Sitting on a hill overlooking the Sea of Galilee, my mind flew
to the feeding of the 5,000 and of course, *"the boy"* (Mark 6:30ff).
It was like reading the familiar story in Technicolor! As my habit
is, I caught the picture in my own fashion.

The Boy

Here is a boy:
A small boy,
An "all" boy.
He's off to hear Jesus preach –
And maybe see a miracle.
Instead he gets to "be" a miracle…

"My, what a lot of people," thought the boy, wriggling his
way to the centre of the crowd so he could see. Then he heard

"the Voice". At first, it sounded like a waterfall — no, no — more like a wind — yes, like a wind in the tops of the trees.

The small boy looked at the trees on the hillside. They were still as still could be, yet it sounded as if the wind blew! The words the Voice spoke were simple — so very simple, but he remembered his Father saying that the Truth of God *is* simple…

So that

All

May

Understand!

The high, the low, the clever, and those that lack knowledge — the old, the young, yes, even the young — like a boy — a small boy, an *all* boy!

The boy's father was right!

Because something's simple doesn't mean it's not *simply profound!*

The wonderful day passed.

The boy was hungry. It was way, way past lunch, but no one had wanted Jesus to stop teaching the wonderful Words of God in order to eat. Until now…

Suddenly everyone was sitting down in little groups and a man, quite rough and ready, appeared as the small boy was unpacking the lunch his mother had sent with him.

"What do you have there, boy?" the man asked. Then, "Come with me!"

And so the boy did.

Now he could see "the Voice", and Jesus, whose voice it was, repeated the man's question, "What do you have there, boy?"

"Oh my," thought the boy, "I've got a hunch he wants MY LUNCH!" The boy had the strangest idea that Jesus hadn't needed to ask the *"What do you have there?"* question. That he knew all about the loaves and fish – that he had even counted them

That Jesus of Nazareth –

A poor man, who'd come to make many rich.

A meek man, who'd come to make many strong.

Knew exactly all about everything. (Which, of course, He did!)

The God man who'd come to save the world, smiled and, just for a mighty moment, the world stopped for a child – and the small boy, the *all* boy gave Jesus *everything* he had in his hands.

Not one fish and a couple of loaves (like we do).

Not half a loaf – not leftovers.

He didn't *share* his lunch with Jesus. He *gave* his lunch to Jesus.

Yes! He gave it "all"!

What a wonderful word is *"all"*!

Can you join me in a prayer?

THE BOY

Lord, you have counted out my loaves and fish. You know
the resources you have entrusted to me. If I am to be
useful to you and others, you need "all". Then, blessed
and broken, you can give me to a multitude of need. I am
in your hands. Help yourself, Lord Jesus!

Amen

BAREFOOT IN MY HEART

NAZARETH

*R*EAD MATTHEW 2:19–23.

Jesus spent many years in "nowhere" Nazareth. Theologians call this time "the silent years". We know He did no miracles, for the one in Cana was the "first" (John 2:11). He spent His silent years serving. Serving His family and His community as a small businessman, a wonderful carpenter.

Do you live in Nazareth? This is the place to learn your trade, to learn to love your neighbours as yourself. It is your chance to let the Divine transform the dreary routine, and make every day count.

Learn of Me

Learn to live in Nazareth,
Learn to ply a trade,
Learn to simply love your world:
That's how a servant's made.
Learn to walk the narrow way,
The road to Calvary,
Learn to take your cross along
And die on it for me.

Lean on Me

Learn to walk the narrow way,
Learn my heart and mind,
Learn to let Me break your heart
For suffering, lost mankind.
And learn to lean for help and strength
Upon my shoulder strong,
Beneath the praise of angels
Learn the servant's song!

Live in me

Then joy in My redemption,
My love, My peace, My grace;
Enjoy the secret garden,
Where we meet face to face.
Know faith in full exuberance,
My presence deep within,
My life and resurrection,
Where too long death has been.

৵৸৶

Have a conversation about *your* Nazareth.

BAREFOOT IN MY HEART

*S*TUART AND I HAD JUST FINISHED teaching hundreds of missionary and pastoral students in seminary training in India. My last message in chapel concerned Moses and his renewed call to service after forty years in the wilderness. Read the account in Exodus 3–4.

The bush burned with fire yet was not destroyed, and Moses turned aside to see this strange sight. When the Lord saw that he had done this, He called to him out of the bush, "Moses, Moses! Take off your shoes for you are standing on holy ground." The fire in the bush was the fire of God.

There ensued a divine conversation that had worldwide repercussions for the kingdom of God on earth! Moses was feeling sidelined, defeated, shamed, and guilty. He had killed a man and fled from Pharaoh's wrath. God had gone to so much trouble training Moses in Pharaoh's palace for his life work delivering the children of Israel from bondage and taking them to the land promised to Abraham.

But the devil attacked Moses through a character weakness. Temper! In fact, all through his long life he was brought low through an uncontrolled temper! He literally broke the Ten Commandments because he lost his temper! Read about it in Exodus 32:15–19. (You always break the Ten Commandments when you let your anger control you instead of you controlling your anger!)

This had led to self-imposed exile while the people of God suffered incredible brutality at the hands of the Egyptians. However, failure is never final for the servant of God, and so one day the Lord, concerned with His people's suffering and wishing to deliver them, met Moses in his dry and barren place of failure and defeat, and the great adventure began. We thought about Moses' story that week as I spoke to the students about the call of God on all of our lives and the fact that failure along the way is never final for the believer.

This was India, so according to custom I slipped off my shoes every time I entered the sanctuary for the lectures. I lived barefoot in those days. Teaching the students barefoot greatly focused my attention on the story of Moses and the burning bush where God renewed his call and commanded him to take off his shoes because he was standing on holy ground! I have been thinking of the many lessons I, the teacher (and hopefully the students), have learned!

It is only when *we* live "barefoot in our hearts" that we will hear our renewed calling to ministry. It is only when we live barefoot in our hearts that we will know the true fear of God and be suitably in awe of the great God we serve, and wish to obey his calling however hard it is. And it is there, barefoot in the presence of His holiness, that He will give us the courage to go where He wants us to go and do what He wants us to do. Here is a prayer I wrote at the end of my talks. I left the words with the students so they could make them into a song and remember the "lessons" of the bare feet.

> *Barefoot I bow at this altar of grace,*
> *Barefoot and humbled with tears on my face;*
> *Ashamed and repentant, I hear the Lord's voice,*
> *Barefoot and humbled, He gives me a choice.*
>
> *Holy the ground where the promise is made,*
> *Keep the fire burning, Lord, don't let it fade.*
> *Help me obey You despite all my fears,*
> *Help me to serve You the rest of my years.*
>
> *Barefoot, accepting Your plan once again,*
> *Give power for my fainting heart, peace in my pain.*
> *Deal with the darkness, give strength for my days*
> *Barefoot and humbled I offer you praise!*
>
> *Barefoot I bow at this altar of grace,*
> *Barefoot and humbled with tears on my face,*
> *Ashamed and repentant, respond to your call*
> *Barefoot and humbled, I give you my all!*

Why not stand before the Lord, right here, right now. Slip off your shoes wherever you are. Listen! Can you hear your name? He is calling you. What will you say?

Holy the ground where this promise is made,
Keep the fire burning, Lord, don't let it fade.

BAREFOOT IN MY HEART

FEELING NECESSARY

SOMETIMES YOU CAN READ the same passage of Scripture for most of the week, or even the whole week. Let's do it together. Read Psalm 139. This is a great psalm for you if you ever feel irrelevant!

Day one, start at the beginning, with the first verse. "O Lord, you have searched me and you know me." Try going to sleep every night thinking of the verses you read during the day. Before I go to sleep, I sit on "the steps of my soul" in "the deep place where nobody goes" and talk with Him about the words we read together. This is the gist of the conversation we had together:

> *"Lord, everyone around me seems so sure of themselves*
> *– confident, knowing where they're going. As if they are*
> *loved, loved, loved. As if they have someone in their lives*
> *who wants to be there for them, who really cares. Someone*
> *who wants to be there when they need to be held, when*
> *they can't stop crying. Lord, it's horrible when you can't*
> *stop crying. When you're not in control."*
> *"I want to be there for you, Jill. I'll hold you! Feeling*
> *irrelevant is more common than you think." More*
> *seriously, He added, "No child of mine needs to feel*
> *unsure of themselves, not knowing if they are loved or*

wanted. I knew you before you were 'you' to know you know! I've known you forever!"

Then I thought of another verse of Scripture that followed that wonderful thought – try to think of other verses that reinforce what you are reading. The verse I thought about was: "What is man that you are mindful [mind-full] of Him?" (Psalm 8:4). How incredible! And I went to sleep thinking about our wonderful conversation, feeling known, loved, planned for, and, above all, necessary!

- Try it. Go on. Read a few verses, such as verses 1–6 of Psalm 139. That should take care of your bad sense of self-worth!

- Capture one sentence about what you just read and thought about in your journal. Perhaps have a conversation about it.

- Go to sleep thinking about the verses. In the morning, see if you can remember what you had your conversation about the night before.

"IF I RISE ON THE WINGS OF THE DAWN, IF I SETTLE ON THE FAR
SIDE OF THE SEA, EVEN THERE YOUR HAND WILL GUIDE ME, YOUR
RIGHT HAND WILL HOLD ME FAST."

Psalm 139:9–10

READ PSALM 139:7–11.

The verses above are surely for travellers! Nervous ones – like me! If you knew how many times I have been in the air this last ten years… So you can get an idea, Stuart and I have been in the States for an average of three months a year. The rest of the time we have had the privilege of taking the "wings of the dawn" and settling (for short stays) "on the far side of the sea"! This verse has steadied my anxious heart on so many flights, so many times! I have felt the grip of His hand on my life! "Even there" as verse 10 says, even there He has held me fast!

> *"Lord, thank you!"*
> *"My pleasure."*
> *"Your steady grip on my soul when I've felt the plane*
> *lurch or struggle against the elements is like nothing else.*
> *And yet I still don't feel safe flying!"*
> *"I know. Thank you for going anyway!"*
> *"I was overcome!"*

BAREFOOT IN MY HEART

"Thank you for asking me to," I replied quietly.
"My pleasure."
"I wouldn't have missed it for worlds, Lord," I said after
a while just being quiet thinking about this conversation.
"To know 'the Holding' is to know what it is to
experience Your power – that force by which all things
consist or hold together!"

I spent some time remembering all the times in these ten years of travel in ministry that I have reached out in fear or apprehension in a plane and found myself, then and there, gripped by the Godhead, sheltered in grace, and unbelievably alive, well, and calm in His encircling arms! But where else would I be?

These verses from Psalm 139 are worth committing to memory! Why don't you write them out and put them in your handbag or briefcase, or on the fridge, or if it's appropriate, on your desk at work? Maybe they would be a blessing to someone else who spends a lot of time "on the wings of the dawn"! Why not write them on a card and send them along? Do it today!

THE HOLDING

OUR NATIVITY

"FOR YOU CREATED MY INMOST BEING; YOU KNIT ME TOGETHER IN
MY MOTHER'S WOMB... I AM FEARFULLY AND WONDERFULLY MADE."

Psalm 139:13–14

OMEONE ONCE SAID DAVID prepared a song about *our*
nativity. It is Psalm 139.

Today, read verses 11–19: "I am fearfully and wonderfully
made!"

Time for conversation!

*"I read in your book, Lord, that light and darkness are as
one to You. It says 'there is no darkness in You at all'."*

*"I am light my child," He replied. "I see you, care for you,
plan for you. In fact, I have created you to perfectly fit the
purpose I have in mind for you."*

I thought about that as I lay in bed in the darkness one night.
It's a great thing to make a habit of reading Scripture before you
go to sleep. Try it! Lay your head down on a pillow of Scripture!

I was comforted by believing that although I was conscious
of the darkness, the darkness and light were the same to Him! He
could see me however dark the darkness was!

I was also overwhelmed by realizing, "He made me on
purpose." He made you on purpose too! This will take care of any

feelings of insignificance we may have won't it? It should!

How do you and I know we are loved by God? One reason dawned on me after reading this wonderful song that David the psalmist composed about our nativity! One indisputable answer is "because He took such a lot of trouble making us"!

> *"You made me IN THE DARK!" I burst out. "In such a small studio with no light! But then David just reminded me, Lord, 'the dark and light are both the same to you'."*
>
> *"I made all the delicate inner parts of your body and knit you together in your mother's womb," He replied. He was suddenly closer than breathing, nearer than hands and feet. I didn't want the moment to pass.*
>
> *I bowed before Him then and thanked Him for making me so wonderfully complex! "Your workmanship is marvellous and how well I know it," I whispered. "I love you Lord!"*

After our conversation I put the light on, got up, and went to my bookshelf to get another translation of the Bible. It's a good idea to collect different reliable translations of the Scriptures so you can read slightly different uses of words that really say the same thing. Truth is rather like a diamond. One diamond, many facets. Just turn it to the light and you see another facet of the same truth. The same truth explained with a different word. For example, "Thou knowest me through and through: my body is no mystery to Thee, how I was secretly kneaded into shape and patterned in the depths of the earth. Thou didst see my limbs unformed in the womb, and in thy book they are all recorded; day by day they were fashioned, not one of them was late in growing" (Psalm 139:15–16, NEB).

A Christian doctor once told me that this aspect of our making was particularly amazing to her. The fact that, in the womb, all the body parts grow at the right rate and at the right time and stop growing at the right time, too! Only God! Remember, we are "fearfully and wonderfully made"!

Another doctor, a gynaecologist, told me that human genes are programmed to "knit" according to an incredible pattern – there are trillions of cells in the body, each containing three billion packets of information – in order to get everything in the right place: eyes, toes, neck, arms, everything!

I looked at my doctor friend, and we both wondered greatly at the Creator's incredible care for us. How could we ever doubt His love?

At peace in the darkness that I knew was light to Him, I said, *"Thank you Lord, for I am indeed fearfully and wonderfully made! How great are you, God."*

Then I slept, content and excited all at the same time, for He made me on purpose, *for a purpose*. He wrote about me in His book. He created who I am for what He had in mind for me to do.

He said so! "Every day ordained for me is written in your book, Lord, before one of them came to be!" It was enough!

Maybe you need to have a conversation about these things? Perhaps tonight before you put the light out and go to sleep?

Thinking Time

Spend some time thanking God for creating you.

Praising Time

Praise Him for "who" you are and how God has made you.

Action Time

In the light of all you have read in Psalm 139, what connection should there be between how God made you and what you could be doing for Him? Finding out what this means means finding out the gifts and talents He graced you with, and giving Him the chance to use all of them in His service will bring fulfilment, give you a sense of purpose, and a reason for living and for dying!

I MADE YOU ON PURPOSE

I made you on purpose.
You knit me together,
You promised Your presence
Come wind or come weather.
I'm the work of Your fingers,
You say I'm your "poem",
You made me on purpose,
And You're leading me home.

I need to stop running
And hold myself still,
My heart needs to listen
As you tell me Your will.
Though the road may be rough
And the way may be wild,
You made me on purpose
And I know I'm Your child.

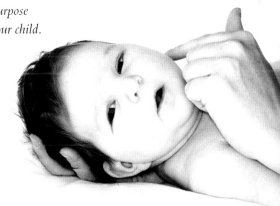

So broken and contrite,
I'm sorry for me:
For my fears and my phobias
That are so plain to see.
But it's never too late
To trust and obey,
And walk home together
And hear Your voice say:

"I made you on purpose,
You're mine in that hour
When I make up my Jewels
By my Almighty power!
So come live in the Glory
And hear Angels' praise,
For I made you on Purpose
For Eternity's days!"

BAREFOOT IN MY HEART

ON THE WAY TO SOMEWHERE

"SEARCH ME, O GOD, AND KNOW MY HEART; TEST ME AND KNOW
MY ANXIOUS THOUGHTS. SEE IF THERE IS ANY OFFENSIVE WAY IN ME,
AND LEAD ME IN THE WAY EVERLASTING."

Psalm 139:23–24

READ PSALM 139 VERSES 19–24.

In Psalm 139:19–22 David identifies with the Lord's judgment on those who hate Him. "Will not the Judge of all the earth do right?" (Genesis 18:25b). There are wicked things perpetrated by wicked people happening in our world. Aren't you glad that one day all wrongs will be put right? I am. Meanwhile we have a choice to identify with Him in His eternal purposes for His people. We can choose to walk in the Everlasting Way and invite others on the road to "Nowhere" to join us.

Perhaps you would like to send this poem, and prayer invitation, to some friends?

I'm on the Way to Somewhere, where "few there be that find",
While many travel nowhere, on the road of lost mankind.
They hope it's leading somewhere, if only they knew where,
But when they get to Nowhere, they'll find that no one's there!

Ghosts instead of people, spirits with lost souls,
No one there has substance, no one's really whole.
Horrors shrouded darkly, nightmares come to be,
When they get to Nowhere – hell's reality.

On the road to Jesus, light and laughter reign,
On the road to Somewhere life begins again.
All who come to Jesus find healing rich and rare
On the way to Heaven, finding meaning there.

The broken will be mended, the crooked shall be straight,
Believe it's true, then walk right through the Way, the narrow
  gate.
Enter at the crossroads: through the crucified,
Thank Him for redemption, the reason that He died!

❧

Find yourself a quiet place. "Be still." Can you think of the words to tell Him you're ready to start life in the "Way Everlasting"? Let me help you. Borrow my words. Make them your own.

> *Lord Jesus, I'm on the road to Nowhere. I know it in my*
> *heart. I've been looking for the way to meaning and life. It*
> *seems in "my world" that everyone is happy to be on their*
> *own road. Happy going nowhere. If Jesus is right when*

He says there is only ONE way to God, it's horrifying
to think of those I love on the certain road to destruction.
But I can't believe for them, only for me.

So Jesus, hear me: here I am. Jesus, here You are! I believe
You are the Way, the Truth, and the Life and no one
comes to the Father except through you! You said you are
the gate that leads to life. I want life – eternal life. Your
life! Please give me Yourself by your Spirit. Right here:
right now!

Thank you, Lord, for hearing this prayer. Now help me
believe and behave my belief. Use me, Lord, to tell others
about the Way Everlasting.

Amen

If you asked the Lord for His salvation today, thank him and write the date in your journal.

Find Psalm 139:23–24 in the Bible. Write in your journal what these verses tell you. Share your discoveries with a friend or family member.

THE DWELLING PLACE

HE SECRET OF SERENITY in hectic and difficult times is something the whole world is seeking and not finding, unless it finds Jesus Christ. Once His Spirit is in residence within us, peace of mind – a feeling of security, of being "held" – becomes a reality.

Moses had more reason than any of us to feel insecure, restless, and afraid. He had no home of his own for years, yet knew a sense of "home-ness" in his heart. He was also able to sing a song about a peace of heart and mind that only God who is our refuge can give. Here is a piece from the Scriptures, which I hope blesses you and reminds you of this truth in uncertain times with plenty of reasons to need a sure and certain inner refuge.

Read Psalm 90, a prayer of Moses the man of God.

Now look at two verses, one from this psalm and one from the New Testament. "Lord, you have been our dwelling place throughout all generations" (Psalm 90:1) and "Now the dwelling of God is with men, and He will live with them" (Revelation 21:3). If you think of a refuge this suggests the same idea. "The eternal God is your refuge and underneath are the everlasting arms" (Deuteronomy 33:27).

"He that dwells…" incorporates the idea of "sitting down and having a rest," not just physically but spiritually, too. Yet many

Christians are tired inside. Have you noticed? The world without Christ is on its feet. There is absolutely nowhere for its soul to sit down. That's why you can be sure the soul of an unbeliever is pacing up and down within, weary of it all. It should not be so with us.

We who profess to know Jesus Christ as Saviour, Lord, friend and brother, empowerer, and lifter of our head: we of all humans inhabiting this little spinning planet should testify to having found an *inner* resting place. We Christians should be sitting down, while the rest of the world is standing up! Does your soul need to sit down? To "dwell in Him" means that we are those whose soul is in repose, and know how to rest in faith and take the weight off our feet.

Years ago when I was working with kids from outside the church, a boy who had recently come to Christ was in my house with a group of his friends and we were studying the book of Hebrews. The book was new to them and to me! We were all trying to get to grips with it. We only had the King James Bible in those days and so we were struggling with the old English words. Trevor, a new convert to Christianity, haltingly read from Hebrews 4, "There remaineth therefore a 'rest' to the people of God." He then asked, "What does this mean?"

I did my best with this, coming, I am sure, far short of the correct interpretation. We struggled to describe the "rest" of faith in the heart for the Christian. In the end Trevor said, "Maybe it's like when Jesus came into my life. It was as if I'd been holding my breath all my life and then I let it out!" I think Trevor had caught the idea of inner rest and peace well. He was talking about the "dwelling" or the sitting down of the soul in repose.

There was so much to discourage those new Christians that the writer of the book of Hebrews was addressing. So much turmoil outside their troubled lives. But it was very obvious to those watching that inwardly they were "resting" in their relationship with Christ. Someone has said, "Discouragement is a tired soul with nowhere to sit down." The believer in Jesus ALWAYS has somewhere to sit down!

Reading Psalm 90 led me to have a "conversation" with Him who is my dwelling place.

> *"Lord," I said, "I'm weary in well doing!"*
> *"Sit down, my child."*
> *"I don't know how! I run so fast hither and yon, and I may be sitting down on the outside, but I'm standing up on the inside!"*
> *"I see you! Tell your soul to settle down on the steps outside My 'front door'. We will talk of these things."*

And so I told my soul to stop frantically rushing around and to listen to Him. It took a while! In the end my soul saw it was no good and I was going to stay there with Him for as long as it took to realize His presence, and so it joined me. It has to you know – we are sort of attached! Finally my busy soul just stopped! What a relief.

THE DWELLING PLACE

"You're dwelling!" He said.
"I know! Dwelling is rest realized internally, isn't it,
Lord? A rest that only You can bestow. Thank you!"
"You're welcome!"

In that moment "we" – me and my soul – knew it was just as He said it would be. He indeed is our "dwelling place" and we were "home".

Do you know this rest? Talk to Him about it. Ask Him to help you to experience Him as *your* dwelling place. Write your conversation in your journal.

GETTING OFF MY FEET

෨෨

TRAVEL A LOT. THE OLDER I GET, the more I find I need to
get off my feet. Standing greeting people after a meeting, I begin
to look around for a chair. Kind folk, often total strangers, are
increasingly saying quietly to me "Don't you want to get off your
feet?" Well, I guess when you see an elderly lady like me hanging
on to a bus strap or in a crowded railway carriage, you remember
your grandparents and rise to give up your seat. (It still happens
occasionally – usually in Europe!)

Not too long ago I was getting out of a taxi to go into a
country club fundraiser and speak for a prison ministry I was
involved in. I got out of the back of the car and the driver prepared
to pull away. I hadn't collected all my stuff from the back seat
before he began to take off. "Stop," I exclaimed, "I haven't got… I
need my… my… I can't do without…" He turned round and saw
me frantically gathering "stuff" I had scattered all over the back
seat. "Walker?" the driver asked helpfully. I was struck dumb, but
only for a moment! "No," I snapped, "computer!"

I felt bad afterwards! But the incident reminded me of how we look at others. Here's an old person who needs help. She has white hair and needs to collect her walker from the back seat! She needs to sit down in a crowded train. She needs to find somewhere to rest. I need to help her get off her feet!

That's right. You and I, whatever our "spiritual age", need to help each other to "dwell" a bit – to get off our feet! "Dwelling" is an internal experience that only the disciple of Jesus really knows; they can know a rest within the soul that only God can give. The rest that you experience when you realize there are works for Jesus that only you can do! This little book will help you connect with the God who has the very best plan for your life. Once you have discovered this, even though you will be working hard, you will experience a calm in your inner being – your soul getting off its feet.

Are you a follower of Jesus? Ask Him to help you experience His internal rest. I did:

> *"Lord, it's good to be 'at home' in You! Thank you, for making this possible. My soul needs a rest – needs to get off its feet!"*
> *"Then do it."*
> *"Really?"*
> *"Really!"*
> *"Right here: right now?"*
> *"Where else?"*
> *"Thank you, Lord. I should have come sooner!"*

Once you're literally off your feet and having a break, reach for your Bible. Read Hebrews 4. Make a list of all the things that stop us entering the "rest of God". Is there anything here that you need to change? Begin the dialogue.

WONDERFUL WORDS

"He who dwells in the shelter of the Most High, will rest in the shadow of the Almighty."

Psalm 91:1

☙

What a wonderful word is "dwell". The word here means "sitting" and has the idea of resting at home. Literally "sitting in the secret place". Most of us have a favourite chair or couch where we can sprawl and relax at the end of a stressful day. Does your soul need to sit down and have a rest? Do you need to take your soul in hand?

Psalm 91, (which is a companion to Psalm 90) tells us that the Lord is our "dwelling place". We can find our home in Him finding rest eternally, and internally, even when externally we find ourselves in deep trouble. We can "be at home" in God.

Who amongst us can know this experience? The psalmist talks about "he who dwells". This is a characteristic of the believer. Of one who is soul-weary and has found his or her way home to the heart of God. He has come home, is at home, and can live in this happy state right here in this unhappy world.

❧

Has this been your experience? Would you like it to be?

Tell Him you would like to know this experience for yourself. Maybe you would like to write your own response, or "climb into mine" and make it your own.

Almighty God, my soul is so downcast, so discouraged, and seems to have nowhere to sit down. Your Word tells me it is possible to come home to Your Heart, and that You, O Most High and Holy One, will receive me, forgive my sin, and settle me down internally. Bring me back to You, I pray, right here, right now! Thank you, Lord. What a wonderful word is "dwell".

Amen

WONDERFUL WORDS

POEMA
"A WORK OF ART"

"FOR [YOU] ARE GOD'S WORKMANSHIP, CREATED IN CHRIST JESUS
TO DO GOOD WORKS, WHICH GOD PREPARED IN
ADVANCE FOR US TO DO."
Ephesians 2:10

LOOKING THROUGH MY OLD JOURNALS I found something I wrote shortly after coming to Christ. It was about my experience in high school and my first year at college. I was often left out of sports teams and the choir, and was never invited to represent the school. Some other girl always seemed to be chosen first. If no one in my world considered me worth choosing for anything, then I reckoned I mustn't be worth anything much.

What would it be like to be "chosen", "singled out", "trusted" with something special, I wondered? When I was in the last year of school I hoped I would be chosen as a prefect. I was in the running but another girl won the privilege. She was picked first. What must it be like to be picked first, I wondered? I fell in love regularly with different boys but when the time came for the dances at school I was never asked by the boys I liked. And the boys who *did* ask didn't choose me for *myself* but because my dad was well off, or they wanted to get to know my sister! I wondered what would it

be like to be chosen, set apart for a responsibility – for a special task – and what about being loved just for myself?

Then one day the living Lord Jesus came to me and forgave my sin. He became my Saviour. He told me I was *worth dying for!* Can you imagine! He gave me His book to read. Oh, the joy that was mine to read His Word and discover His grace and love. It said in His Book that he had work for me to do. He had chosen me before the world began to do this particular work. No one else would do, only me. How much better this was than even being chosen to be a prefect for my elite school! It was shortly after this that I began to keep a diary of my conversations with Him in a journal. The following is one of them. I called it: "Consider Yourself"

Consider Yourself

> *Grace filled His horn with oil [for anointing] and came looking for me. He found me at Cambridge University, in hospital busy being sick.*
> *"You are the one," He said. "Consider yourself chosen."*
> *He poured the consecrating oil of The Holy Spirit into my life – "consecrating".*
> *"But I'm only a first-year student teacher," I muttered.*
> *"I know."*
> *"I don't even get As (and not always Bs)," I said honestly.*
> *"And I wasn't chosen for the tennis team again this term."*

"I know."

"And Lord, I'm the youngest in my family. And have you noticed, Lord, my sister is much prettier than me?"

"I know. I made her!"

"Well, nobody of any importance has ever singled me out before," I explained, "so it's sort of hard to believe."

"I'm Someone Important don't you think?" He replied. "So consider yourself anointed!"

"But anointing sounds so grand — isn't it for missionaries or nuns or, er, kings and queens?"

"Consider yourself 'royalty'," He said softly.

He put His hand under my chin and made me look up. Then I saw He was smiling at me.

"Consider yourself loved." He said ever so gently.

And so I did. And life began. Joy!

All these years later, I find myself meeting many people who feel just like I did. For all sorts of reasons, we feel worthless, useless, hopeless, and helpless. It could be you were mishandled as a teenager, or abused as a child. It could be that you have been disappointed by a life that isn't fair. Maybe your spouse left you. It could be you have lived in the shadow of a brilliant sibling or tried in vain to live up to the high expectations of a parent. "What's the point of me trying to do anything significant?" you ask yourself. "Who'd want me anyway?"

He wants you! He loves you! He has plans for you!

POEMA

Being in India among the Dalits – the poorest of the poor and the lowest caste – in a system that doesn't always value women, caused me to teach three things. One, you are chosen; two, you are loved; and three, you are anointed. In places where women are devalued this special teaching brought light, life, and liberty.

Do you consider yourself chosen, anointed, and loved? Did you know He picked you? You were first on His list for the work He had in mind. He has a job just for you! Yes, he does. What's more He believes you can do it. "For [you] are God's workmanship, created in Christ Jesus to do good works, which God prepared in advance for us to do" (Ephesians 2:10).

What joy I experienced in India, meeting the devalued, the deceived, and the downtrodden – who are coming to Christ in great numbers – and showing them from the Scriptures that they are chosen, loved, and anointed for service of the King of Kings and Lord of Lords. And then to see these same people taking their lives and making them count for good and for God in difficult and often dangerous places.

Of course, you don't need to be a Dalit or a woman in India to feel devalued and worthless. You can feel like that in the good old US of A, the UK, South Africa, the Middle East, or anywhere else in God's green world!

But listen to me. You were worth dying for, planning for, equipping with precious spiritual abilities, and being called to do a work that He wants "only" you to do.

Consider yourself a "Poema". You are precious to Him!

❧❧❧

Write a paragraph in your journal about this. Perhaps you could write a letter to Him expressing what you feel about yourself. Then write out the verse of Scripture from Ephesians 2:10. Memorize it!

POEMA

PEACE MY MIND

THE PHONE CALL CAME EARLY on a bright morning. It seemed strange because the sun was shining, the birds were singing their happy songs, and all appeared right with the world! The voice relayed the message crisply and clearly. Bad news: worse, bad news that was true! Not a horrible rumour or malicious gossip: true facts. After I carefully put the phone back in the cradle, I began to move.

First I put on the TV – loud. Then I started cleaning the oven (it didn't need it), sorted though old clothes to give to the charity shop, and cleaned out a cupboard in the basement that was in perfect order. After rushing around for quite a time, I slowed down and just began moving aimlessly around the house.

After a bit (actually quite a bit), I began to talk – quite loudly, as I was alone in the house.

"Lord, someone has done something that has shattered me. I don't know where to put myself. I can't sit still. See me just wandering around the house wishing it was time to go to bed and sleep so my stomach would stop churning, my mind would stop running around like a frightened rabbit, and my heart would stop beating so fast."

Then I heard it. The VOICE. It's unmistakable isn't it? And I could hear it above all the human noise I had bombarded myself with to try to drown out the voice I had just heard on the phone! (How silly is that!)

The Voice said, "Be still!"

> *"How can I 'be still' when my whole being at this moment of distress is racing round and round? If I keep moving, maybe I can outrun the reality of what I have just heard, Lord. Maybe I can outrun the trouble that's coming on the heels of the news: escape —"*
>
> *"You cannot escape this situation. It is! Now, be still. I Am! Stop it! You cannot 'know' the reality of my saving presence until you stop this."*
>
> *"I can't stop! It's not fair that you should say 'stop it' when I can't!"*
>
> *"I wouldn't tell you to if you couldn't, that wouldn't be fair."*

Well now, what can one do after *that*. Somehow, I'll never know how, I obeyed. I sat my soul down on a chair — and I sat with it and said very sternly, "Don't get up until I tell you to!" It sulked — but obeyed — it will, you know, if you insist.

In that desperate moment, I lifted my arms to Him who is my Father — like the child that I was.

> *"Father, Father," I cried. "See this wound so deep and raw. See my spirit crushed. See my spiritual lungs*

gasping for breath."

"I see."

"Hold me, Father, hold me!"

My Father God took this shattered woman in his arms and held her so very tightly. I remembered then – imprisoned in His saving arms – that, blessing the tribes at the end of his life, Moses had said: "underneath are the everlasting arms" (Deuteronomy 33:27). He should know! Being held that close to His heart helped me to hear His voice more clearly.

"I am God"

"I believe!"

"Be still. Just KNOW it, right here right now."

After a time, I have no idea how long – it could have been one minute, or ten, or thirty – I knew!

"All is well," my heart whispered. "All is well!" How strange when all was not! "Only You can do this Lord!"

"Only I can."

After this, the words came, words asking Him for the help I was going to need.

Darkest shadows feeding fears,
Panicked mind and scalding tears,
Nothing like this down the years,
Peace my heart, O Lord.

Lord of peace and calmness still me,
May your Holy Spirit fill me,
Lord, this pain would try to kill me,
Save me, help me, Lord!

Touch and mend my raw emotions,
Devil's stirring up commotions,
Cannot think to have devotions,
Centre me, O Lord!

Speak your loving, gentle healing
To my mind beyond all feeling,
Stop my thoughts, confused and reeling,
Anchor me, O Lord.

Give me God-thoughts, wisdom needed,
Show me Scriptures never heeded,
Help me then apply this balm,
Chase away this deep alarm,
Help me lean on your strong arm,
Steady me, O Lord!

God sufficient, strong to save me,
Strength and hope and wisdom gave me!
Thank you, Jesus, that you found me,
Angel voices all around me
Lift my Spirit, Lord, astound me –
Holy Heavenly Lord!

PEACE MY MIND

Are you in shock? Have you just received some really bad news? Where are you? What are you doing? Are you saying as I was saying:

> *Darkest shadows feeding fears,*
> *Panicked mind and scalding tears,*
> *Nothing like this down the years?*

Then why not borrow my words to start your own heart talk? Say, "Peace my heart, O Lord."

Or you could read the psalms of Moses – Psalms 90 and 91 – and maybe memorize some verses. Perhaps these words could help a friend in trouble? Pray about this. Give them a Bible with a bookmark at these passages.

MIRACLES TAKE TIME

Recently as I waited for a miracle, a poem was birthed.

Waking to Grace at the light of the dawn,
Feeling depressed and a little forlorn,
Needing a miracle,
Needing it now,
Impatient and worried, I bow.

He'd answered before, but His voice now was stilled,
I needed so badly to hear what He willed.

"My child, I have heard the heartbeat of your pain,
And at the right moment, I'll answer again.
Take this time to know Me
In a way never known,
I'll explain when I get you back home!

"Then you'll praise Me and see from the heavenly sphere
That the timing was right, though the pain was severe.

You would never have known what My Presence could be,
If you'd walked not this hard path with Me."

MIRACLES TAKE TIME

Then settling in to His plan for my days,
I looked for His working in miracle ways,
And one day I saw both the rhythm and rhyme
Why His miracles sometimes take time!

No less a miracle if we have to wait
Till we enter Eternity's gate!

Stuart and I were at a conference listening to the amazing reports of missionaries from New Tribes Mission telling their stories. It was a real-life adventure of how they had taken their families, moved in among unreached primitive people groups, and begun the years of persistent and patient language and translation work required to take the gospel and plant a self-reproducing church. It takes years to learn culture and language, win the hearts of the people, gain credibility and trust, in order to translate the Bible and bring the gospel of light to dark places.

To establish a presence, gain acceptance and then start the work of discipleship cannot be done short term, just as mission work cannot be done at arm's length! A ministry of "presence" (or "being there") and patience is required. And it takes a dogged determination to stick to the task and wait it out.

Years ago we served with a youth mission. Our leader had a saying, "Go where you're sent, stay where you're put, and give what you've got!" We were told by the leaders of New Tribes Mission that they had the same philosophy and that the hard task in our

day and age is the middle part: *"Stay where you're put."* It takes a certain set of the "spiritual chin" to stay put in such primitive places. I could well imagine how difficult it must have been to "stay the course" working with the tribal people groups until the goal was attained.

There is no way round it, no short cut, even with technology unknown to the founders of this wonderful mission. This incredible venture, this hard and dangerous work, takes time. Lots of time. It means taking on the hard work of "waiting"; sometimes waiting it out in life-threatening situations.

For us Westerners, waiting for anything is akin to suffering. We want everything now, if not sooner! Sometimes we catch ourselves giving up the patience thing and calling for a miracle. Doesn't the Bible say we can move mountains with prayer? Doesn't Jesus promise, "Ask, and you will receive, that your joy may be full" (John 16:24, ESV)?

At the same time as I was listening to these wonderful servants of God giving their reports of their translation work, I was preparing to speak at a C. S. Lewis convention and had been reviewing some of Lewis' famous quotes. As I worked on my presentation, I was reminded of something I had gleaned from Lewis' book, *Miracles* – "miracles take time". The words "miracles" and "time" seemed at first thought to be an oxymoron. At second thought, it dawned on me that here was a truth that could help me. After all, Jesus Himself was proof of it. Think of the incarnation. That miracle of miracles took time – nine months!

When Stuart and I first came to America we learned we had the oldest oak tree in Brookfield in our front yard. As we sought to raise our three teenagers to know and love the Lord in a strange and unfamiliar culture, I would go outside, look at the towering tree and pick up some acorns to put around the house to encourage my heart. "It takes time to grow an oak tree," I would remind myself! I think I heard a whisper, "Hope on, miracles take time, yet a miracle that takes time is no less a miracle than one that takes no time at all."

Have you been pleading for God to intervene in, say, a child's life? A child perhaps who is making bad choices? Are you praying for instant godliness, for quick transformation? Are you waiting for a marriage to heal? For a miracle of reconciliation or instant forgiveness of all hurts and wounds inflicted? Let me paraphrase Dr Lewis Smedes' helpful advice in his classic bestseller, *Forgive and Forget*:

> *Human beings forgive best one hurt at a time. And that can take a while. A long while! Only God can forgive everything at once! And we are not God. Usually the miracle of extending forgiveness to someone who has wounded you deeply, doesn't happen overnight.* [1]

In other words, "miracles take time".

Are you trying to discover the will of God for your life? It's a miracle in itself that God "has" a plan for our little lives! Are you impatient for the Lord to lay it out in one grand "life calendar" on your iPhone? The whole deal? The details? The very next step, the middle, and the end as well?

This is not to say miracles cannot happen all in a moment of "human time". Of course they can. Follow Jesus' footsteps through the Gospels. Watch Him bring instant health and healing; cast out the demon, transform the soul. I have experienced it, and others bear witness to it. But God's clocks, I have learned, keep perfect time. I must keep my little fingers off the face of His "timepiece" and trust Him with the schedule. The Bible tells us, in "the fullness of time… God sent forth His Son" (Galatians 4:4, ESV). There will be "a fullness of time" for us too, according to His wisdom and knowledge.

However, God, unlike us, is in no earthly hurry. His purposes transcend our little clocks and watches. And I'm glad about that. Be encouraged. Who knows what I, and those I pray for, would lose if we received instant answers to our prayers. Certainly our character would lack lustre and our faith remain weak.

Persist. Pray on and on and on. Don't lose hope. Ask for your miracle, of course, and then trust God for it according to His will and in His time.

Years ago, I wrote in my book, *Prayer that Works*:

> *"Ask Him to do it but don't tell Him 'how'.*
> *Ask Him to do it, but don't tell Him 'now'!"*

One day you will be able to look back over many months, or even years, and in retrospect see the love of God in the puzzling delays. In the words of one of my favourite hymns:

> *"Hast thou not seen*
> *How all thy longings have been*
> *Granted in what He ordaineth?"* [2]

≈≫

Does a personal talk on "the steps of your soul" seem necessary? Be still. Read this piece again. Begin the conversation.

MIRACLES TAKE TIME

ACORNS

"VERY TRULY I TELL YOU, UNLESS A KERNEL OF WHEAT FALLS TO THE
GROUND AND DIES, IT REMAINS ONLY A SINGLE SEED. BUT IF IT DIES,
IT PRODUCES MANY SEEDS."

John 12:24

෨ඏ

TWO WEEKS' MINISTRY IN AUSTRIA and Germany in springtime set me to worshipping the God of creation. The incredible view from the Schloss, a beautiful ancient castle that houses one of the Capernwray Bible Schools and a conference centre for young people, was particularly fine from our bedroom window – 200 steps from the base of the castle to the top. That, along with the steps to get there, took our breath away! Then on to Germany, where Stuart and I met with Russian Christians of German descent, most of whom were immigrants who had come back to Germany from the former Soviet Union in 1989 when the Berlin Wall came down. They were wonderful people, worshipping in burgeoning church fellowships across the land.

One day during my stay I was looking for something in my purse and my fingers found an acorn I carry with me as an illustration for one of my talks. Looking at the little nutty seed (or fruit) and then at the trees around me I thought of the vibrant,

young Bible school students, and the godly "Russian Germans" who had returned to plant churches across Germany. With their strict Baptist faith intact, honed into usefulness through years of Communist domination and persecution in the lands from which they had come, they were busy planting evangelical fellowships and passing on their faith to the next generation.

Jesus' words from a lesson in John's Gospel came to mind: "unless a [seed] falls into the earth and dies, it remains alone; but if it dies, it bears much fruit" (John 12:24 ESV). The principle of "dying to live" remains the same today. In this season of ministry I met many delightful "oak trees" who surely delight the heart of God. They certainly delighted me as I listened to their stories and realized there had been a lot of "dying" going on before the "new trees" rose triumphant from the soil.

The young men and women who came to the meetings we had in Europe practised a self-disciplined, self-giving, and sacrificial lifestyle for Jesus' sake. Many had died to their own ambitions and dreams in order to train others for Christian service. Some had put their personal plans and relationships on hold in order to give themselves to mission work. There had been a lot of dying going on in order to see such evident spiritual life.

There is no other way for all of us, I reminded myself. The frightening thing is that "we little nutty acorns" have a choice. "To die or not to die, that is the question."

He whom I love was listening to my soul thinking. So I wasn't surprised when I heard the question:

> *"So what will it be for you, Jill?"*
>
> *"Well, Lord, the problem is, if I'm honest, I'm really very fond of myself. I don't like pain!"*
>
> *"So then, what will it be? Self-preservation at all cost?"*
>
> *Oh dear! I knew He wouldn't let me away with talk that just went nowhere.*
>
> *"Er, I need to pray about it!"*
>
> *"You are!"*
>
> *"Well now, I suppose I am!"*
>
> *"So what will it be, Jill?" The still small voice can be very persistent can't it?*
>
> *"Will dying hurt?"*

Silence. The Lord doesn't bother saying anything when He knows you already know the answer! I knew the answer, and He knew I knew. All dying hurts, but not as much as trying to live life without the dying! In the end that hurts you most of all. I knew the biblical principle in my head: "You die to live, you give to get."

> *"Lord," I said, (to gain a little more time and put off the*

moment of truth and action) "I'll… I'll think about it —
er — write a poem about it!"

So I did. I called it "Acorns". It was quite good, I thought, so I was hoping He would be pleased with my creative work and let me off the hook!

Acorns

> *Think of an acorn, then look at the tree:*
> *Who would have imagined what it could be?*
> *So inconsequential a seed in the earth*
> *Lying buried and broken — yet waiting rebirth!*
>
> *The birds of the air find a place for their young*
> *A cathedral to practise their songs yet unsung.*
> *The canopy covers the creature who's caught*
> *In a wintry rainstorm of the very worst sort!*
>
> *The branches are perfect for feathered friends' nests,*
> *The squirrels find pathways, the small birds find rest;*
> *Our human eyes wonder at tree trunks so tall,*
> *And we praise God our Father and Maker of all.*
>
> *But we like our brown colour and hard little shell,*
> *And we're scared of the dying: we'd rather stay well.*
> *While some die to themselves and never look back,*
> *Others hide in their cases, just too hard to crack!*

ACORNS

So the choice is our own as to what we shall be,
To remain as a nut or become an oak tree!
We can die to ourselves, be reborn and survive,
And find in the dying that we come alive!

I looked at Him hopefully. I'd prayed about it and written a poem about the subject, hoping that would be enough. I even had a talk coming up in church to a class of women who needed to hear the principle of "dying to live" and I decided I could include it in this.

> *"Nice poem," He said mildly, "so when are you going to do it?"*
>
> *Bother!*

That was the problem with my Christian life. I knew the truth: wrote about it, prayed about it, and even had the nerve to teach the truth to others, but at the end of the day I was still very much alive! The self-centred Jill wanting to continue with the self-centred, self-absorbed, self-aggrandizement that I was choosing to live. It was time to stop all the talking and just DO IT!

I went outside and found an oak tree. The hard conversation He and I had there is too private to share, but He told me that part of our talk might help someone else and to pass it on.

> *"Lord, I said in the end, I'm a nut!"*
>
> *"Your choice!"*
>
> *"I want to be a tree. Tell me again, is there no other way than dying?"*

"No other way."
Then in a very quiet voice, half-hoping He wouldn't hear
me, I said, "I'm ready – scared – but ready!"

I went inside and found a hymn book I keep at my bedside – it contains some great devotional hymns of the faith – and borrowed the words of a verse of one of my favourite ones, "Take My Life and Let it Be".

> *Take my will and make it Thine—*
> *It shall be no longer mine;*
> *Take my heart – it is Thine own,*
> *It shall be Thy royal throne.*[3]

I stayed still, and at last there was a cracking of the hard, brittle shell that had been keeping me such a small hard shape and size for so long. Somewhere inside me, life began to sprout and spread and grow, pushing upwards towards the "Son".

It would take a lifetime to grow to my full spiritual height, of course. But after this conversation, I stood often under that great oak tree in my garden greatly wondering at my reluctance to submit to dying for so long. Fresh green growth pushed its way out of the seed of my small faith and life renewed!

❧

ACORNS

Walk outside and find some trees. (Maybe, like me, you'll find an oak tree.) While you're out there start a conversation: say what needs to be said and listen to His Word, then do it!

The "dying to live" principle is one Jesus Himself talked about. You can find it in John 12:20–30.

Read through the passage three times. Sometimes it takes more than a cursory reading to connect with the text. Ask questions of the text. See if there is one main thought that strikes you as pertinent to your life at this time. What is it? Write it down in your journal.

- What did the principle of "dying to live" mean to Jesus? Have a conversation about it.

- Write down one thing He "said" to you from these words. Often you "hear" His words in your thoughts.

- Buy a hymn book to add to your devotional library. You can turn hymns into prayers.

- Thank Him for the day ahead.

- Think often of the words that have passed between you and the Lord. Pass them on.

SO MANY THORNS

"MY GRACE IS SUFFICIENT FOR YOU, FOR MY POWER IS MADE
PERFECT IN WEAKNESS."

2 Corinthians 12:9

☙

MY MEDITATION after reading Paul's words in
2 Corinthians 12:9.

She'd been given a problem of personal pain,
And she'd prayed He would heal it again and again.
He asked her to bear it for God and for good,
So she stopped her petitions and said that she would.

As soon as she asked for His strengthening Grace,
He showed her His hands and His side and His face.
The marks in His head were so jagged and deep
That she couldn't keep looking and started to weep.
So many thorns in the brow of God's Son,
Yet He only asked her to take and bear one!

His grace was sufficient,
His strength her enabling,

His peace beyond reason He gave her to know
His touch in her spirit,
His light in her darkness,
His presence He promised: "Lean hard as you go."

"My child," He said gently, "drink deeply of grace,
Lean hard on my shoulder and finish your race."
So many thorns in the brow of God's Son,
Yet He only asked her to take and bear one!

So she "leaned" and was strengthened, as promised by Him
Who'd overcome Satan and trouble and sin.
The knowledge of God she experienced that hour
Was worth all the tears as He gave her His power.

So many thorns in the brow of God's Son,
Yet He only asked me to take and bear one!

WHAT ELSE IS THERE?

❧

T was sitting in a rocking chair in our 1840 schoolhouse, a cup of tea and my Bible close at hand. He and I had been talking. It was time to be interrupted by the world and his wife.

I didn't want to be interrupted and I didn't want our time to end. But life goes on, doesn't it? I was glad I had started the morning like this. Just Him and me. I couldn't see when we would have had the chance to talk in a very busy day. Not real, leisurely talk as if we had all the time in the world. Yes, I was glad. "Glad" is a great feeling! "I'm glad you're glad," I heard Him say as the world arrived in the shape of people needing breakfast.

"What else is there?" I murmured. And again, as I got going in the kitchen, "O dear Lord, indeed, what else is there?"

> *What else, save time at your feet,*
> *A pause in your presence,*
> *Time holding its breath with this sense of "Everness"*
> *pervading my living room.*
> *Holiness that hovers, evidenced by quietness beyond quietness*
> *permeating the room? Who else is here save You, Lord?*
> *I know not anything or anyone to compare.*
> *In the end, "What else is there?"*

WAITING

"How long, O Lord…?"
Habakkuk 1:2

෨෨

*T*HIS PRAYER POEM WAS MY response to reading the book of Habakkuk. I hope it will help you reflect on the text too. Read the prophet's words – it's only a short book.

Waiting for the dawn to dawn when night is long and black,
Waiting for a heart to heal or a child to get on track.
Waiting for delay to end and wishes to come true,
Waiting for a sight or sense of You.

Waiting for the one who left to find the way back home,
Waiting for this sense of loss to leave my heart alone,
Waiting, wondering, hurting, in a hole of pain so deep,
Waiting for just one good night of sleep.

Waiting for an answer, for evidence that You care,
Waiting for employment, for just one answered prayer.
One small affirmation: for freedom from self-doubt,
Waiting for a way to work it out.

BAREFOOT IN MY HEART

Waiting for the Bible to start to make some sense,
I'm sick of my ambivalence and sitting on this fence.
Waiting for a promise that truth will have its way,
For justice to win out one grace-filled day.

Waiting for a world that's deaf to hear You and repent.
Waiting for the human race to believe the One you sent
To save, forgive, equip to live in holiness and power –
Waiting for salvation in this hour.

Waiting for the violence and the conflict that abounds,
The wrong You seem to tolerate, the injustice that's around
To stop, because You intervene and answer desperate prayer:
Waiting just to know You're waiting there.

But Lord, the waiting's killing me, I cry to You for peace,
To still the storm inside me and make all this turmoil cease.
Help me to remember as I try to do my part,
How patiently You waited for my heart.

You waited for repentance that was Your perfect due,
You waited out resentment and my anger aimed at You.
You waited in the shadows and You offered me Your hand
To strengthen me to wait it out and stand.

WAITING

So however long the waiting lasts, as long as You decide,
I'll stand upon my watchtower and I'll climb my
    mountainside,
And I'll ask you, Lord, for "hind's feet" and my soul will
render praise,
As You and I will wait for better days.

Though the fig tree does not bud and though no cattle are in
    the stall,
Though donkeys and the sheepfold have no company at all
Yet see my heart, O Sovereign God, rejoicing in your grace:
Content to wait it out and see your face.

BAREFOOT IN MY HEART

LIKE A HART UPON THE MOUNTAIN

"THE SOVEREIGN LORD IS MY STRENGTH; HE MAKES MY FEET LIKE
THE FEET OF A DEER, HE ENABLES ME TO GO ON THE HEIGHTS."

Habakkuk 3:19

෮෨

AFTER READING THE LAST FEW VERSES of Habakkuk, I spent
time on "the steps of my soul" thinking about being like "a hart
upon the mountain". Then I scribbled a poem prayer, and left it for
Him in "the deep place where nobody goes" as a small expression
of praise for my redemption. "I love you Lord!"

> *Like a hart upon the mountain*
> *With water on its mind,*
> *Like a squirrel in the winter*
> *Without some nuts to find;*
> *Like bats without a belfry*
> *Like a wedding with no ring,*
> *Like a bird that's flying upward*
> *Without a song to sing.*

Like a girl with none to marry,
Or a man with none to wed,
Like an orphan with no parent,
Like a child that can't be fed.
Like a sick one with no medicine,
A poor man without hope:
Like a single parent, desperate,
Without the strength to cope.

Like these that I've just mentioned
I was in such a case,
Then God in Christ revealed to me
His loving, saving Grace.
He showed me how He'd suffered,
For my little life to save:
And He told me I could come to Him,
And my lost soul He'd save.

Now like hart upon the mountain
I drink from clear streams,
Like a child who suffered nightmares,
I have the sweetest dreams.
As bird with crystal-clear song
Delights the listening ear,
Like a poor man with new confidence
Who has nothing left to fear.

BAREFOOT IN MY HEART

I'm a person now with purpose
And I'll be Christ's little hart,
I'll leap and run, pure symmetry,
And play my little part.
However vulnerable I am
The Lord will rule my days,
And like a hart upon the mountain,
I'll bring Him boundless praise.

❧

Read Habukkuk 3:17–19 and write Him a note of praise, or add your own verse to the poem.

BAREFOOT IN MY HEART

SELF-AGGRANDIZEMENT

❧

*A*MEDITATION ON HABAKKUK 3:17–19 before preaching at a church.

> *"This mountain's fraught with 'self' traps. Please, Lord –*
> *hind's feet, give me hind's feet."*

The internationally respected preacher and Bible scholar the Revd Dr John Stott once said, "The pulpit is a very dangerous place for any son of Adam." I would humbly add, "Or for any daughter of Eve."

The apostle Paul's injunction was to live after the Spirit, obeying His instructions and keeping in step with HIM, and not to live after the "flesh". The intent of the flesh is panic and fear or, on the other hand, self-aggrandizement and self-trust. The intent of the Spirit is to impart peace in the panic, power to the timid, serenity – the "tranquility of order" – to the heart and fitting humility to the soul.

Living in the flesh is a given – we have no option. We were born in sin. Living *after* the flesh is an option that in the power of the Spirit we are expected *not* to take!

> *Frightened, worried, tired of trying,*
> *Smile in place, inside I'm dying,*
> *Hardly coping, losing ground,*
> *I'm listening Lord, but hear no sound.*

In this moment make me whole:
Freshen faith and mend my soul.
Humble heart and mind and will
Bid my soul be quiet and still.

Climbing on the highest mountain,
Drinking from the Spirit's fountain.
Hind's feet kept from trips and slipping,
Conscious He my hand is gripping.

Stretching, growing, Jesus knowing,
Faith releases, Spirit flowing,
Self forgetting in my walking,
In my service, in my talking.

Made like Jesus may I be,
Saviour, help me honour Thee.

Make me a blessing, Lord.

BAREFOOT IN MY HEART

LOSING HEART

᷾HIS STUDY COULD TAKE YOU a few days or just one day. You could even do it in one day at three different times. That way you could receive blessings at breakfast, break-time, and bedtime!

"Therefore we do not lose heart," says the apostle Paul. "Though outwardly we are wasting away, yet inwardly we are being renewed day by day" (2 Corinthians 4:16).

Read 2 Corinthians 4:7–12. What a wonderful passage! What does Paul say here about his ministry? Make a list in your journal.

Now read Judges 7. When Paul uses the illustration about jars of clay in 2 Corinthians he is probably thinking of this Old Testament story about Gideon fighting the Midianites. Why do you think Paul uses this picture?

What helps Paul to renew his life with God? See 2 Corinthians 4:16.

Have you ever lost heart? Do you ever suffer from "heart failure"? This world of hate, destruction and hopelessness, is too horrible, too cruel, too unfair. People let you down. It's a terrible thing to lose heart. Ask mine!

Paul experienced all sorts of troubles. Enough to make him really miserable. But even though all these things happened to him, he is still able to say that he *does not* lose heart. Here is what I gleaned from this passage to help myself. You may find altogether different things if you follow my example.

Keep your eye on the "big picture"

What did Paul do so he didn't lose heart? He remembered what life in Christ was all about. He didn't get lost in the minutia.

Retrace your steps

When you have "lost heart" ask yourself, "*Where* did I lose it?" Paul retraced his to the trouble that caused him to be discouraged.

Whenever I lose my glasses (all the time) Stuart tells me to "retrace my steps". It's the same when I lose my car in the airport car park and the nice policeman who knows me so well kindly sighs and says, "Miss, you need to think back to when you came into the car park. Where did you enter?" I need to retrace my wheels!

Go back in your mind to the place you lost heart. The very place. Go on, visit the place when you became aware of "the dead air" in your devotional time, for example. As Amy Carmichael put it, "the sense of 'miss' that overcomes you, when something is missing." Something very important. When you are honest and say, "I lost something… my heart," go back in your memory to that incident or conversation. You'll find your heart there. Oh, it may be lying flat on its face gasping for air, but it will be there. It will need reviving, of course. For that renewal there will be God's part, and your part!

Thinking about this I sat still and then asked the Lord, *"Lord, is there an example of someone losing heart in the Old Testament?"* I gave it time until the Spirit brought David to mind. When reading the Bible it's good to stop and think about the teaching, the verses, or examples. I turned to David's Psalms and read until I found Psalm 42. This is what I found on the subject there.

Make your heart listen

Read Psalm 42.

One day David stopped his hurried heart hurrying and sat down for heart rest. At once, his heart collapsed in a flood of self-pity. David's heart hurt: he was heart weary. So many evil men had been hunting David like an animal. He was tired of the running, the hiding, the fear, and never sleeping properly. Of waiting for the enemy to find him and finish him off. We can be like that too.

What did David do? David made his heart sit down and listen to him. Then he made it listen to God. He said to his soul, "Why are you downcast, O my soul? Why so disturbed within me? Put your hope in God, for I will yet praise Him, my Saviour and God" (Psalm 42:11).

Perhaps Paul had been thinking of David when he was writing 2 Corinthians 4. Did he say to his heart, "Poor us! It's not fair [which it wasn't], it's too much [which it was], I'll just lie down and die [which you can't, you know, however much you want to]?" No, he sat his heart down and asked it some hard questions, just like David had done, telling it to shape up and start hoping again.

I thought David's idea was really good. I thought of the time my hurting heart needed a rest. I went to "the steps of my soul" and found a place in "the shadow of the Almighty". My heart lay there gasping for breath. It was "blue in the face". I realized it was having a heart attack! Well, I could have called for the heavenly ambulance, but I knew the medic would hand me the instruments and make me do the procedure to revive my own fainting heart. So, like Paul, I decided to try David's method.

"Why are you giving up on me, heart?" I asked it. Then I said, very robustly and loudly, to make sure it heard me, "Take heart, O heart! God is on your side."

It answered. "But I am in this deep hole. It's so dark and I have arrhythmia! I feel I'm being buried alive."

"See Him who got up from the grave and walked out of the tomb. He will strengthen your heart. IF YOU LET HIM!" I said severely. Then I began to exhort my failing heart with strong words, just like David did. "Stand up, heart." I said. Go on! Stand up! What are you doing down on your face? Are you beaten? Worried? Discouraged? On your feet! You are in the presence of resurrection life! Stand up, O heart!

"Look up heart! Go on. Look up. See the clouds part and the sun begin its rising. Does not His book say, 'He who regards the clouds will not reap?' (Ecclesiates 11:4, ESV) Speak up, heart.

Speak to your God. Tell your words out loud. Say it heart. Cry out to Him. Keep up, faint heart. He goes before you. He will meet you around the corner of your dread with a great new hope for a whole new day."

After a little while my heart got up, took a deep breath and said, " I will yet praise Him. Let's go!" And so we did!

⇛⇝⇨

Pick a verse from any of today's readings to meditate on. Memorize it before you pray.

This prayer time should be easy. Do what David did – talk first to your soul and then to God!

Write down your "best thought" after this study and meditation. Pass it on to anyone you know who's losing heart.

LOSING HEART

SMILE ON ME

Smile on me, Lord, see me here,
Bending low in reverent fear;
Frightened, sorrowed, here I bow,
Meet me in my darkened now.
Smile on me as chaos reigns,
Come to me, release my chains;
Lift my head and let me see
You, my Father –
Smile on me,
Smile on me,
Smile on me!

Know that God looks towards us in grace. He is smiling not frowning. He loves us even when "We have done those things that we ought not to have done." Don't be afraid. Look up!

FINDING

"I KNOW THE PLANS I HAVE FOR YOU," DECLARES THE LORD, "PLANS
TO PROSPER YOU, PLANS TO GIVE YOU HOPE AND A FUTURE."

Jeremiah 29:11

෨෨

READ JEREMIAH 29:11–14.

This was God's promise to His people in Old Testament times.
A promise to the exiles in Babylon that He would bring them back
to Himself, back to the Promised Land, and back to the plans He'd
given to Abraham. They were to be a missionary nation so that all
the world would be blessed through their message of a Saviour.

Did God have a plan only for Israel? Or does this promise of
blessing for the future apply to all of God's people and those who
will believe through their witness? I believe His promise of "hope
and a future" refers to all God's people down the ages, including
the church of Jesus Christ!

But does God's grand plan for the world coincide with mine?
Even once I'd come to Christ, I still had wonderful plans for my
personal life! I found myself musing, "Could God's plans be better
than my personal plans?" How silly is that? How could God's plan
not be better than mine!

The problem comes when we realize God's plan may result
in trouble, pain and problems, whereas those things are seriously
absent from our plans for ourselves! But didn't Jesus say to his

disciples: "In the world you *will* have trouble" (John 16:33)?

Yes, He did, but He also promised we could laugh at all the dark days that might be ahead and say loudly, "greater is He that is in [us] than he that is in the world" (1 John 4:4 ASV). Again He said, "Be of good cheer; I have overcome the world" (John 16:33 ASV). God's plan for His people is to engage in His mission. Each of us has a precious part to play in God's grand cosmic plan and that plan supersedes all our own little plans and dreams.

I was a new Christian, only eighteen years of age with the promise of my whole life to live and news that God had dreams for my life excited me, but the idea that those plans would include darkness and suffering, deprivations and broken dreams terrified me. I had a choice to make. To choose His dream come what may, or mine.

This was worth a conversation. I remembered the talk I had had with the Lord in "the garden of grace" one morning long ago. It went something like this.

> *"Lord, I have dreams, the dreams of finding fame and*
> *fortune. The dreams of life lived out in my beloved*
> *England. Of finding the love of my life, and having kids*
> *and family togetherness. Of course," I added hastily, "we'll*
> *go to church and volunteer quite often, as well – when we*
> *can fit it in!"*

To be honest, my ideas of serving Jesus were serving *where* I wanted to serve and *when* I wanted to serve. Fitting God into my plans.

*This was the day I heard His voice asking, "Whose plan
is it to be, Jill? Mine or yours?"*

I realized I didn't want to give Him my dreams in exchange
for His for me in case they didn't match my secret hopes.

*"What if I let 'Your' dreams for me come true, Lord?" I
asked. "What happens if my dreams are never realized?"*
"One day you will be glad."
"When?"
*"When you decide to care only about my plans and
purposes for your life and give up your own."*

I wondered greatly if I would get to care at all about His
plans when I cared so very much about my own. It was then that
I found to my consternation, I didn't really believe His plans *could*
be better than mine!

*"It's up to you what you believe," He said quietly! There
now, He hears all our thoughts! I was embarrassed.*
*"Lord, please don't let it be up to me. You choose," I
begged. "It's just that – that – the devil is telling me if I
let You choose, my dreams will turn to nightmares!"*
"Who are you going to listen to – him or Me?"
"Er – that's really scary!"

So He and I sat on "the steps of my soul" and had a long
talk about it. It was one of the most important conversations of
my life. In the end, I decided my dreams were so much safer in
His loving keeping than in mine. I should not be listening to the
devil's opinions and, anyway, I couldn't make dreams come true!

So I relaxed, wrote a poem, and said a prayer:

> "Lord, if not one of my dreams come true, so be it. I ask
> that I may fulfil your dreams for me, which actually may
> include doing without mine! That's all right, Lord! I love
> You. I trust You to know what is best for my life. Amen."

I called my poem "Finding".

Finding

Giving up my dreams of grandeur
Finding sweet relief,
Seeing plans of self-promotion
Only brings me grief.

Laying down my dreams of riches
Finding He will care
For my basic needs of living –
He will answer prayer.

Giving up my dreams of family,
Precious from the start,
Finding that He cares and comforts
When He has my heart.

Taking up the cross of Jesus,
Only then to see
A vision of His loving purpose
Finding dreams for me!

FINDING

Great and far the wide horizons
Wait to be explored,
He would have me find the vision
Of my Risen Lord.

He it is that gives me insight
Of the human race,
Lost and lonely, happy only,
Finding saving grace.

Dreams have turned to living nightmares,
Children hurt, distraught;
Satan finds them, takes them captive
Blinds to truth that's taught.

May they trust a Risen Saviour,
Finding Jesus cared,
Take me, make me, bend me, send me
Where they've never heard.

May they find deep peace and healing,
Comfort, purpose, sight:
Grace and love from up above,
Fulfilment, joy and light!

BAREFOOT IN MY HEART

FINDING

Is it time for you to have a deep conversation about these things? Don't put it off. Your life is waiting! Write a little of your talk with the Lord in your journal.

FOREVER TIME

⁓

> "What time is it in Your world, Lord?"
>
> "Forever!"
>
> "Of course! It's a quarter past seven here on this little spinning planet."
>
> "I know."
>
> "Time to begin a day in my world. What day is it in Your world?
>
> "Forever day."
>
> "Oh. What's that like? Living in Forever? Living in timelessness? A sphere where it's never a quarter past seven?"
>
> "Wait and see."
>
> "I guess I'll have to!"
>
> "Just a little time now, Jill."
>
> "I love the way you say 'Jill'!"
>
> "Wait till you hear me say it in Forever!"
>
> "O Lord!"

After this conversation I was reminded of a verse about Israel; I remembered it was in Isaiah's book but I didn't know where exactly. When that happens I get a concordance and look up a word or phrase I *can* remember in the text. So I looked up "name",

the word I could remember (I could have looked up "mine" too).
I soon found the verse I wanted: "I have summoned you by *name;*
you are mine" (Isaiah 43:1b).

A name is such a personal thing isn't it? And what a wonderful
word is "mine"! Especially when you hear *Him* say it! Aren't you
happy when someone remembers your name? And when someone
loves you very much somehow when they say your name it sounds
so different from when others use it.

Does my conversation remind you of another verse in the Bible?
Find the verse in a concordance. Write it in your journal and talk
to Him about it.

DEEPLY GOD

I WAS READING AN OLD BOOK in which the writer used the phrase, "God is deeply good." I don't know why but it touched me. God is indeed "deeply good" because He is "deeply God". There is no fathoming the depth and height and width of His being. Yet in all His great God-ness, He can, through the ministry of the Holy Spirit in our hearts be "deeply known"!

(Don't forget to use your journal when you study the Bible and meet with the Lord. One thing you can capture is a phrase – as I did here with "deeply good". If you don't write the thought down somewhere, you'll lose it.)

Do you ever feel a trifle shallow? Dare to let Him deepen you in every dimension of your life – your life with Him and your service to others. *Go on, let Him!* Tell Him you are ready for the "deepening".

God is "deeply kind", whereas I am deeply unkind. God is "deeply compassionate", whereas, if I'm honest, I really don't care about anyone else but me! Do I dare to ask Him to take me deeply into the eternal secret of who He is and what He desires to do about all my "deeply bad" stuff?

Go on, ask Him! If it helps, borrow my words.

Deeply God and barely known.
Here in pain and all alone:
Hurts my spirit, cries my heart,
Knows despair that tears apart
Small belief and knowledge light,
Knowing not what's wrong or right.

Give me inner eyes to see
How "deeply good" you've been to me!
See the depth of sin and shame,
See the traps of pride, of fame,
Deeply needing humble thoughts,
To be a servant as I ought.
Deeply sorry for my sin,
Make me what I should have been.
Go as deep as needs be,
Take my heart and deepen me.

Deeply needy, hear my prayer,
Broken, desperate for repair!
Deeply needing change inside
Where Your Spirit now abides.
May I filled with goodness be:
Deeply made, Lord, more like Thee!

BAREFOOT IN MY HEART

One thing I have discovered is that the deeper I go with God the more "heart" I have for people without Christ. When I was a young Christian, I found myself caring deeply for people, especially young people: kids in danger, at risk. I began to work with unchurched young people in my hometown streets. It was a whole new world to me and soon I was overwhelmed with the need. I required help, but everyone was busy with their own things and didn't seem to care. I turned to some biographies of people who had had a similar ministry to keep me going.

Some people find it hard to read anything. I suggest you try reading missionary stories: the lives of Hudson Taylor, C. T. Studd, Gladys Aylwood, Mary Slessor. Stories keep the attention, especially true stories. In these books I discovered real people who chose to let God take them deeply into His will for their lives. We can learn from them how this relationship with the Lord can work for us.

When I was young in the faith, reading true life stories gave me a "heart hunger" for more of God and widened my understanding of what it means to "go out on a limb" in serving others. These unmet mentors (men and women I met in the pages of these biographies) birthed in me a love for a lost and desperate world. Phrases or quotes from these books went into my journal and have been good companions on my faith journey.

The writings of Amy Carmichael have shown me how to find help from the Scriptures in times of need, and there is a quote from one of her books, *Fragments that Remain,* that I have returned to down the years. It has to do with a time at the start of her ministry, when Amy and a handful of workers were rescuing little girls from temple prostitution in India. It showed me how to use my Bible to have a conversation with God in prayer in order to find help, especially when I was discouraged with too much need around me and too few people who were moved enough to help.

> *In the days when hardly anyone cared whether the children perished or not, I used to open my Bible and read aloud as a child would to one who is very near and listening, "There went with him a band of men, whose hearts God had touched" (1 Samuel 10:26). And I used to say to our God very longingly, "Where are they, Lord, those hearts You have touched? You know that I cannot go to look for them. Look for them for me, O Lord, my God, Father of these little ones, great Toucher of hearts."*
>
> *How the ancient stories live! "There separated themselves into David men of might fit for the battle… — then David received them and made them captains of the band." 1 Chronicles:12:8–18 tells how it was and is.*[4]

Find a real life story, read it, and capture a quote, a lesson you learned, or phrase that touched you. Maybe it will be as this was for me, an example of courage. It could be a true story about the

Christian work ethic, or being called to serve, despite the opposition, while waiting for Him to bring helpers.

Learn more about the person's life, mission, and country where they served. Once the book has touched you, give it away. Pray about who to give it to – give it soon! Then pray that they read it and receive encouragement.

One year, I gave Christian biographies to all my family and close friends for Christmas, and another time for birthdays. Make yourself familiar with a Christian bookstore in your area. Their staff can point you to the right books. Ask your friends to recommend biographies that have helped them. Make a list. Why not collect them to share with others?

DEEPLY GOD

BEING VITAL AND GREEN

"EVEN IN OLD AGE THEY WILL STILL PRODUCE FRUIT;
THEY WILL REMAIN VITAL AND GREEN."
Psalm 92:14 (NLT)

YEARS AGO SOMEONE SENT ME a comment from the famous American writer James Michener. It was about what kept him writing well into his old age. Apparently he said: "When I was forty-five, a farmer living at the end of our lane hammered eight nails into an ageing, unproductive apple tree. That autumn a miracle happened. The tired old tree produced a bumper crop of juicy red apples. When I asked how this happened, the farmer explained: 'Hammering in the rusty nails gave it a shock to remind it that a tree's job is to produce apples.'"

Later the writer said something to the effect: "In the 1980s, when I was nearly eighty, I had some nails hammered into my trunk – heart surgery, vertigo, a new left hip – and like a sensible tree, I resolved to resume bearing fruit."

Nails get driven into all of our lives, especially as we get older. They can cripple us or they can jolt us into using our maturity and experience to make a significant difference for good and for God. This year in our travels, Stuart and I have had some health issues

and ministry challenges, not to mention we've each had one more birthday! That was another jolt!

We have chosen to remember what apple trees are all about. Bearing fruit whatever our age. We don't want to be trees bearing nothing but leaves!

I want to share with you a verse that has become important to me in this season of life: "Now that I am old and grey, do not abandon me, O God. Let me proclaim your power to this new generation, your mighty miracles to all who come after me" (Psalm 71:18, NLT).

Why not spend some time in Psalms 71, 90 and 92?

Time passes but the joy of heartfelt worship abides: "It is good to give thanks to the Lord, to sing praises to the Most High. It is good to proclaim your unfailing love in the morning, your faithfulness in the evening… You thrill me, Lord, with all you have done for me! I sing for joy because of what you have done…" (Psalm 92:1–2, 4 NLT).

I have met believers who are young in age yet old before their time. And I have met old people who are fresh and green through the Holy Spirit's life-giving work in their hearts! They can testify to the truth of Psalm 92 – "A song to be sung on the Lord's Day" – a song about the freshness of spirit and joy that won't quit, which keep us young at heart.

How refreshed we are by your power, Lord:

"You have anointed [us] with the finest oil… the godly will flourish like palm trees and grow strong like the cedars of Lebanon.

For they are transplanted to the Lord's own house. They flourish in the courts of our God. Even in old age they will still produce fruit; they will remain vital and green. They will declare, 'The Lord is just! He is my rock! There is no evil in Him!'" (Psalm 92:10, 12–15, NLT).

> *"You promised me, Lord, if I am planted in your 'garden of grace', my world will see greenness in my life and ministry, and be refreshed by the fruit of Your Spirit."*
> *"I keep my promises, Jill. Now you keep yours."*

REVELLING

ༀ

I revel in Your beauty and I celebrate Your peace,
And as I am obedient I find such sweet release.
I'm passionate to please you and live a life of praise,
So I'll smile at dark tomorrows and sanctify my days.

Ever climbing upward and reaching for a star,
I know no sense of loneliness for I know where you are:
You're living in my ransomed soul, You're filling every day,
So I'll lose myself in loving and I'll give myself away.

I revel in your presence and I celebrate Your grace,
And I want to stay forever and look into Your face.
But now is time for serving and I need to do my part,
So go with me, Lord Jesus, and fill my needy heart!

REVELLING

NOTES

1. Paraphrased from Smedes, L. B., *Forgive and Forget: Healing the Hurts We Don't Deserve,* New York: HarperOne, 1996.
2. "Praise to the Lord, the Almighty", Neander, J. (1650–80); trs. Winkworth, C. (1827–78).
3. "Take My Life and Let it Be", Havergall, F. (1836–79)
4. Carmichael, A., *Fragments that Remain.* (B. Trahane, Ed.) Middlesex, United Kingdom: The Dohnavur Fellowship, 1987